C000001056

Taming

Wealth

of the wicked

Uebert Snr, PH.D

2

Contents

Chapter One

The Greatest Wealth Transfer: The Devil Stole your Wealth!

The devil owns your workplace, your bank and the market place. When you get paid he leaves you with a few dollars to put in a bank he also owns. After you deposit that money into a bank he owns, he will force you through circumstances to withdraw that money so that you spend it on paying bills and buying necessities. The problem still is that he also owns the market place where you buy your necessities. But with Jesus as Lord of your life - the period of the devil owning the company you work for, the bank you bank with and the market place where you buy your goods is over for the word of God says:

Proverbs 13 Ch 22
...the wealth of the wicked is LAID UP for the believer.

Now, the child of God ought to have God's best. A child of God was rich beyond his wildest imagination, way before he was even created. He was born into the right family. He was born where the money was and still is. He was born in a place of wealth created just for him.

Remember that when God made Adam, the first commandment He gave him was to prosper. It was wealth that God first spoke to Adam. He did not even start by saying 'good morning my son Adam' or 'good afternoon Adam'. Adam rose up from that soil to find God's mouth inches from his nostrils. We would all like to think that God said something different to what He really said but in all God's wisdom He spoke prosperity. He commanded Adam to take over. God said:

Genesis 1 vs. 26-31
...have dominion over the fish of the sea, and over the fowl of the air, and over the cattle, and over all the earth, and over every creeping thing that creepeth upon the earth... Be fruitful, and multiply, and replenish the earth, and subdue it: and have dominion over the fish of the sea, and over the fowl

of the air, and over every living thing that moveth upon the earth..., Behold, I have given you every herb bearing seed which is upon the face of all the earth, and every tree, which is the fruit of a tree yielding seed...And to every beast of the earth, and to every fowl of the air, and to every thing that creepeth upon the earth, wherein there is life, I have given every green herb... And:

After God gave this command to Adam, God said:
...very good...

God said wealth was good. In fact the first commandment the creator said to the created was to have dominion, to multiply and to subdue. It was all about wealth creation and management of wealth. See!

Man wasn't created to be a slave, that is why favour follows him and that is exactly why the people who are not in the kingdom work for their money and heap up wealth without the knowledge that they are doing this heaping up of riches for the believer. In short the people on earth are all working for the child of God. Notice what God does:

Ecclesiastes 2 vs.26
...to the sinner God giveth travail to GATHER and HEAP UP riches that he may give to him that is a believer Of God.

All sinners are by scripture working for the believer whether they or you know it or not.

Notice here, the devil stole a lot of our material possessions but now he is paying and supposed to pay back sevenfold. God has been and still is involved in the business of **making the sinner work to GATHER and HEAP UP riches that will be given to the believer** and by 'believer' I mean the believer who has understood or will understand the revelation of wealth.

The Revelation of wealth

The wealth of the wicked is yours for the taking. Prosperity is our portion as believers. This prosperity *is not just* in houses, cars, nice clothes, jewellery and fat bank accounts for this is where many who preach prosperity miss it; its purpose is so that we having enough will be able to further the spreading of the gospel. It is money with a mission!

The church should not be poor and the child of God should not be broke. We are supposed to have plenty enough to be a blessing to others. Notice here in the Word of God:

2 Corinthians 9 vs.8
> **And God is able to make all grace abound toward you, that YOU, always having ALLsufficiency in all things, (look now at the purpose of riches) may have an abundancefor every GOOD WORK.**

The children of God should not be beggarly. They should have God's best and that is not negotiable. They should have plenty enough to live a brilliant life and plenty enough to help others in need. The children of God should *never ever be beggarly*.

Notice what David said along this line in the book of

Psalm 37, 25, 26
> **I have been young and now am old.Yet have I not seen the righteous forsaken nor his seed begging bread. He is ever...lending and his seed is Blessed.**

David also adds:

Psalm 34 vs.10
> **The young lions do lack, and suffer hunger but they That seek the Lord SHALL NOT LACK any good thing.**

David even rubs it in a little bit further by saying:

Psalm 23 vs.1
> **The Lord is my shepherd I shall not lack Anything.**

Notice, it is high time we start owning our workplaces, the banks we bank with and the marketplace. It is time for the *greatest wealth transfer the world has ever seen.* It is time for the devil to pay back what he stole. The revelation you are holding is *payday for the believer!*

The biggest wealth transfer!

The biggest wealth transfer and money explosion the earth has ever seen is upon us. But we need to be *willing and obedient so we can eat the good of the land* and be able to make the wealth transfer from the wicked to the believers.

God wants you to have plenty enough to pay your bills, live a prosperous life, master money rather than to let it master us and above all your wealth is soul-money - money to win souls with. It is money to help in the furtherance of the gospel. God wants His children wealthy. What father wouldn't want his children to be prosperous? What father wouldn't want his children to abound in every good thing? What father wouldn't want his children to be successful? What father wouldn't want his children to be a blessing to others?

It is God's will for His children to become rich just as it was His will to let the plunder of the Egyptians become a success and it did in style!

You and The Plunder of the Egyptians

Now, this is not the first time for the wealth transfer to happen. To understand wealth transfer, I would like you to look at how God made the wealth transfer from the Egyptians to the Israelites:

Exodus 12 35
> **And the children of Israel did according to the word of Moses; and they borrowed of the Egyptians jewels of SILVER and jewels of GOLD and RAIMENT**

Notice what God did after they asked for SILVER, GOLD and CLOTHES from the Egyptians:

Exodus 12 36
> **And the LORD gave the people favour in the sight of the Egyptians, so that they lent unto them such things AS THEY REQUIRED. And they SPOILED the EGYPTIANS**

The Israelites left with the gold, silver and clothes of the wicked. In fact they left with SUCH THINGS as they required. If you look at verse 35 again you will notice that the scripture says "*...the children of Israel did according to the word of Moses...*", as if it was Moses who said it without the backing of God. However, before Moses got to Egypt and way before chapter 12, God had already spoken to him in chapter 3 and had given him information on what would happen at the exodus of the Israelites. God was behind that great wealth transfer just as He is behind this biggest wealth transfer that is upon us. Way back God says:

Exodus 3 vs.20
> **And I will stretch out my hand and smite Egypt with all my wonders which I will do in The midst thereof: and after that he will let you go.**

Exodus 3 vs.21
> **And I will give this people favour in the sight of the Egyptians: and it will come to pass, that, when YE Go YE SHALL NOT GO EMPTY:**

Exodus 3 vs.22.
> **But every woman shall borrow of her neighbour, and Of her that sojourneth in her house, jewels ofSILVER, and jewels of GOLD and RAIMENT: and ye Shall put them upon your sons, and upon your Daughters; and YE SHALL SPOIL the Egyptians.**

God was in the midst of the plan to run away with the wealth of the wicked. Gold, silver, clothes and all the things they asked the Egyptians to give them. The wealth of the wicked was given to the Israelites in their time as God had promised and now in this day and age God has breathed His revelation to us ward who believe, so as to enable us to make this wealth transfer a reality that will help take the Gospel to the far ends of the world.

This is not something new, it has always been in the word but only a few people took advantage of it. Some taught it and suffered persecution not from the world but from the very pulpits that were supposed to support them. Some used the revelation but then went into extremes and turned into wolves in sheep's clothing. They started stealing from the people of God – bankrupting them whilst they hoarded money to themselves because of greed.

However, the pages you are holding will take you to the very fields of the wealth transfer. They will take you to the land of plenty!

Now, God's will is to prosper you and increase your substance. He has no problem with you driving the best, eating the best, living in the best houses e.t.c He gave the Israelites favour and they managed to ask for expensive minerals and materials from their oppressors and then He also gave them power to run away with them. God's will is for His children to have His best. It is His best for you to have plenty no wonder the word says:

Psalm 68 vs.19
> **Blessed be the LORD, who daily LOADETH us with BENEFITS... SELAH.**

The word SELAH there in verse 19 is a Hebrew word denoting a call to think about what has just been said. It is a word that says *"think about that for a second"*. It carries in it a *'wow!'* factor. This shows the reality of the fact that the Lord actually loads us with benefits daily; spiritual and physical.

Wealth is a matter of choice

However, being loaded with the wealth of the wicked is a matter of choice just as being poor or being rich is a matter of choice. Whilst it is true that there are some who are born rich, this does not mean to say those who are not born rich are not given power to get rich like those who are born rich. As a matter of fact the moment one becomes a Christian they are already exposed to all the material and spiritual blessings known and unknown to men. Remember, *any born again and Spirit filled child of God was rich beyond his wildest imagination, way before he was even created. He was born into the right family.* He was born where the money was and still is. He was born in a place of wealth created just for him to such an extent that there are no more excuses for any child of God to be poor for poverty is a curse. Believers are not cursed. Christ has redeemed us form the curse so being loaded with the wealth of the wicked is a matter of choice!

King Solomon declares this truth, that being poor or rich is simply a matter of choice. He declares that God has given opportunities to those who become rich and those who become poor. The difference is some folks take the opportunities and become rich and yet some ignore and become poor. Look at how King Solomon puts it here in the book of Proverbs 29 vs.13;

The rich and the poor have one thing in common God gave all of them sight.

This is the same thing the scriptures will be speaking of when they say that God is merciful to the extent that He, in:

Matthew 5 vs.45
... sends rain on the just and the unjust...

According to God your being poor is simply a matter of the sight you chose not to use and not where you were born or who you where born to. To God it is a matter of choice and you can choose to ignore the revelation that the wealth of the wicked is up for grabs and definitely yours for the taking. Someone, as they read this will choose to take this revelation and become wealthy with it and use their wealth to spread the Gospel. It is a matter of choice.

Now, if I am to say that for you to live from pay cheque to pay cheque is to deny the power of the gospel, many would be angered by that statement yet notice that there was an anointing in:

Luke 4 vs.18
...preach the gospel to the poor...

A lot of people don't like to look at that because good news to a poor man is that he *doesn't have to be poor anymore* yet believers today are living in absolute financial bondage. Some would say that was not what Jesus was saying, but saying that would be missing it. See!

You need to notice this fact - Jesus was talking to people who already believed were going to be well in heaven so for him to promise good news to the poor 'in heaven' would simply be weakening the truth of why He came. The poor under the Jewish tradition are already prepared to be rich in heaven. Jesus was talking about the good news that they would not be poor anymore, in spirit and physically.

Now many Christians have been brainwashed, taught wrong and need to be re-educated on the subject of wealth. They are living to make a living and by so doing have little time to spread the gospel, which is the *number one mission for every believer*. All the while, Jesus is saying, 'I've been anointed to...**preach the good news to the poor**

Believers have held back the flow. They have short-circuited and denied the everlasting force of power that could deliver them from not only sin and sickness but from the horrible effects of poverty. God is ready to lead believers into the greatest wealth transfer the world has ever seen and when you receive this revelation and make it yours - **the devil will be caught unawares** as you move into the land of wealth. You will start to plunder the wealth of the wicked and beautifully amaze those around you!

The Plunder

Now getting back to the Israelites plundering of the Egyptians, notice something in verse 22 of Exodus 3 that the Israelites were not only told to ask the Egyptians but also the visitors who had visited the Egyptians. God was in for a big take over. He was releasing favour to take maximum wealth.

Exodus 3 vs.22
> **But every woman should borrow of her Neighbour and of HE THAT SOJOURNETH IN HER HOUSE...**

That is increase! All the GOLD, SILVER AND CLOTHES the Egyptians had; God in the spiritual realm considered it STORED UP for the righteous. He was simply waiting until such a time as was necessary to give it to the righteous. God then permitted the transfer, commissioned it and created a time and a way to plunder the wicked Egyptians. See!

You and The New Wealth Take Over

All the banks, companies, land, houses, money e.t.c are yours to further the gospel with. They are Stored Up for the believer to be *willing* and *obedient* like the Israelites were and plunder the wicked. The way God did it then is less of an affair than the way He will employ with you today. Be ready because He is simply waiting for: ...**doers of the word**...to step up and take over the wealth of the wicked.

God in this day and age has a supernatural and legal way that will catch the devil unawares. This way possesses a supernatural speed at which the wealth of the wicked will be taken over in a flash for godly purposes. Simply make yourself available. There is no need for the believer to borrow loans from banks and steal or deal illegally thinking they are taking over the wealth of the wicked. God is not a thief and does not belong to the mafia either!

You might say "**but brother, God plundered the Egyptians by making the Israelites borrow and run away with the money so why do you say He was not robbing the Egyptians**", in a sense you will think you are justified but for us who have studied the words of the bible by revelation and by going back to original languages we understand that the word 'borrow' as put in the King James Version of the Bible will surprise you if you get to know the meaning of it (we will discuss this word later). Before discussing that word let us understand that in this covenant God has a new way for wealth transfer which includes even the old but with a greater power this time and a different supernatural speed.

The new supernatural wealth take over is not for the minority like it was in the time God brought it forth for the Israelites. This time it is for every one who is in the Lord whether white, tall, black, slim, pink, yellow, orange or polka dot.

The word of God says:

Galatians 3 vs.28
> **There is neither Jew nor Greek, There is neither Bond nor free, there is neither male nor female: for Ye are all one in Christ Jesus.**

What God is saying here is that in order for believers to get the wealth of the wicked to be transferred to them so they can call the shots in this messed up world, there is need to do away with sense realm nonsense like " *if I was just white"*, *"if I was just born to so and so"*, " *If I was just black"*, " *if I was just slim or fat"*. That nonsense is a stumbling block to wealth for we are all one in Christ according to Galatians 3 vs. 28.

Who you were born to or whether you were born in a garage is of no importance because when you start moving in the anointing of the wealth transfer, the prophecy of the prophet Isaiah will start to show in your life whether you are white, tall, black, slim, pink, yellow, orange or polka dot.

Isaiah 61 vs.5
**Strangers shall stand and feed your flocks,
And the sons of the alien shall be your
ploughmen and your vinedressers**

The wicked will just hand you riches you did not work for. The Holy Spirit will compel them to give you riches. He will make it happen for you to have favour with foreigners that their sons will work for you for low or no money at all. Ideas for business will come to you from every direction and even when you are on a toilet seat. Anywhere you will be business ideas will supernaturally pop in to you and come to you. This is a supernatural wealth transfer that many will have a problem believing because they cannot imagine it. However the word has an answer to why people will have problems believing and here it is;

1 Corinthians 2 vs.14
**But the natural man recieveth not the things
of the Spirit of God... neither can he know them,
because they are spiritually discerned.**

This wealth transfer is difficult to understand with the mind. It takes a spiritual man to discern the spiritual. The wealth transfer revelation is for those who are spiritually mature. It involves principles that are guarded by God. This is not a *'genie in a bottle'* revelation where you just shout some crazy words like *'shakaka shakaka lalamu'* and wow! money shows up. No it is not. The wealth of the wicked revelation has Holy Ghost directed principles that need to be followed. These principles are tangible steps that have supernatural backing as you shall see in the following chapters.

Is not this wealth spiritual?

Now, a man asked me whether this wealth which is stored up for the just was in heaven only and not on the earth. I answered as the Lord gave it to me. The wicked can not have spiritual wealth for they are sinners. There is no sin in heaven so nothing is stored up that belongs to a sinner. Sinners are not righteous; they have no spiritual wealth to be stored up for them in heaven. What they have are natural resources, riches that control the economies of this world preventing us who preach to spread the gospel for they also own the privilege of the airwaves - television, radio, communication avenues, governments and many other resources that pose as obstacles for the spreading of the word.

The wicked people of this world control this world system. They are very prosperous in their system and use that system to prevent the furtherance of the Gospel. Let's look at:

Psalm 73 vs.3-12
3. **For I was envious at the foolish, when I saw the PROSPERITY OF THE WICKED.**
5. **They are not in trouble as other men; neither are they plagued like other men**
7 **...their eyes stand out with fatness: they have more than the heart could wish"**
12. **"...behold, these are the ungodly, who prosper in the world; they INCREASE IN RICHES.**

The wealth the wicked people have is for selfish purposes and chiefly hinder our progress with the gospel. This wealth is here on earth and not in heaven. There are rich countries in this world that are preventing tooth and nail to let us in with the gospel. These countries do not know anything about the gospel of the Lord Jesus Christ. They would not even recognise the Holy Spirit if he walked down row by row in their parliament with a red hat on.

These countries are rich to the extent that they use their powers to prevent the spreading of the gospel. It is here that the wealth of the wicked will be transferred to us who believe so we can call the shots in those countries. That reason is the answer to why God's first words to Adam had everything to do with prosperity and subduing – He knew something was to go wrong so He said 'subdue' meaning to put down.

The wealth transfer is not so that we can just show off with our Mercedes Benz, Cadillac, Bentleys and jets. No it is not. It surely is money for us to live a good life but chiefly, to ensure the furtherance of the word of God. The scriptures say in:

Ecclesiastes 9 vs.16
...the poor man's wisdom is despised and His words (of the poor) are not heard.

Your image has a lot to do with whom you are going to reach. If you want to win the rich send a rich man or a man of miracles for as you have seen - the words of the *poor are easily despised*. In fact the Lord has no problem with people knowing you are blessed. Look at it here:

1 Timothy 4 vs. 15
Let your profiting appear to all

As you see, blessings from God will give you advantage and favour with people. The poor will attract the poor and the poor in the Lord will hold this revelation of the wealth transfer dear to their hearts. It is liberating.

There is also a need for the focus to always be on the spreading of the gospel and not on wealth.

Maintain Focus When wealth comes

When wealth comes however, we should understand its purpose in order to keep the wealth transfer door open. The purpose is to use our wealth in the soul winning business. *I cannot stress this enough*. It should be for the work of God because if it is centred on just you and not helping in spreading the word of God it will fly away. Notice what is said in:

Proverbs 23 vs.5
for riches certainly make themselves wings, they fly away as an eagle toward heaven.

Understanding the purpose of wealth will let you become a wealth recipient. It will make you a magnate for riches. Wrong focus will make wealth fly away or your love for God to run away. God Himself through the mouth of David warns us in:

Psalm 62 vs.10

>**...when wealth increases do not set your
Heart upon them.**

>**The Lord Jesus touched on this point by equating
money with a master. He said in Luke 16 vs. 13**

>**No servant can serve two masters for either
He will hate the other and love the other or
Else he will hold to the one and despise the
other. You cannot serve God and mammon**

Do you see that God is not saying He does not want you rich? We know this because just before verse 13, the Lord said we should make money. Look at how He put it in:

Luke 16 vs.9

>**And I SAY UNTO YOU make to yourselves
FREINDS of the mammon (money)**

All He is saying in verse 9 is that money is needed then in verse 13 He is saying money should not be the focus so it should not be treated as a master. The whole point in a nutshell is that when money increases do not set your heart on it. So it is okay to be rich but wrong focus is the one that is not accepted.

We should never set our hearts on wealth, but on the purpose of that wealth. See!

Wealth transfer in my life

It was mid 2006, in the small town of Atherton near Leigh in Manchester United Kindom of Great Britain around 5am. I got a visitation from the Lord Jesus Christ Himself. In that vision I saw a great part of the heavens opened and a huge hand meters wide, came out of the open heavens and a voice said to me; "rub yourself into my hand and take the anointing to teach my people how to get the wealth that they will use for kingdom purposes". This is a voice I can never forget. It is a voice I would not stop thinking about even if I could, and would not even if I could. I thought of why God had chosen me. I did as the voice of God commanded in that vision. I rubbed my arms and hands on that mighty hand and a green colour like I have never seen green before was now on my hands so I rubbed it on my whole body and the voice then acknowledged itself to me as the Lord Jesus Christ. He then told me to pray for the household that had hosted me and to teach them some of these wealth transfer principles that morning. This was not the first time I had received a vision. As a matter of fact at the time of this writing I have seen angels more than fifty times and have seen the Lord Jesus Christ more than six times.

When I got out of the vision I informed my wife, spoke to her about the principles I'd been told by the Lord and then I taught and prayed with the couple I had visited about the same things. The beautiful couple acted upon what the Lord had said and *just hours* after that, they received multiple checks made to them from different sources including banks that did not owe them anything. Some just decided to do promotions and apparently they decided that this couple was to be one of the recipients. The following days it started happening to us. People would come to us and just bless us with their substance. Many would proclaim that they were led by God to help us in our ministry and we in turn used and still use the wealth for the purpose of the kingdom. We set our gaze at the purpose of wealth and not on wealth.

"When riches increase set not your heart on them"

The day the Lord Jesus Christ plundered the colt

Some will argue with this and say it is some kind of magic whereas there are spiritual laws that are triggered when a believer obeys God in a certain way. There are principles given in the word that will open the door to the 'stored up wealth'. The Lord Jesus Christ walked in this anointing. We see Him sending His disciples to go and take a colt. The disciples asked what they would say if asked by the owner why they were taking it. The Lord said "say the LORD wants it". The word 'LORD' means *'master owner'* meaning the real owner. All these years the donkey owner kept His donkey and fed it but that day the *real owner* came into the picture and demanded His property. He wanted to use the donkey for kingdom purposes. Someone says but that was Jesus... Yes but like Paul let me answer – It is Jesus...

Acts 27 vs.23
In whose I am and whom I serve.

Notice, the steward of the colt did not even put up an argument. The Spirit of God had to compel him to understand the need of the Lord. Even in this life when you have a purpose to spread the word of God at heart, the Holy Spirit will compel people to help with their substance. He will unlock doors to the STORED up wealth. You know what the word says about giving.

Luke 6 vs.38
Give and it shall be given unto you, a good measure, pressed down and shaken together and running over shall man give into your bosom.

The scripture says if you give, **man will give you,** *not God.* God's duty will be to compel people to give you if you can only obey. For money follows anointing, obedience and not education.

Attracting the wealth of the wicked

Money does not follow education on its own. It is not attracted to how many college or University degrees one has. Wealth is attracted to the anointing. I am *not* against educating oneself. I have a very good education myself. My wife and I studied finance and other degrees at University level and we both received Best student awards in our respective years. At the time of this writing we are Finance lecturers at University level. We are therefore qualified to know for a fact that money is not attracted to a college degree.

There are doctors who live a pauper's life as if they have never been to school. On the other hand there are very rich people who can't even spell their name. Money is attracted to the anointing and anointing comes by obedience. Anointing brings a hunger to know more about money and the wisdom to create it.

Obedience like faith starts were the will of God is known. If one does not believe God wants them rich there will be no fire in them to get rich. Believers should be aware of all the full package of the gospel.

Two sides to the word

There are two sides to the word. Half of it is "the devil comes to steal, kill and destroy..." the other half is that Jesus "...came that (we) might have life and have it in abundance..." all we need to do is to choose our half. Some preachers have chosen "...the devil comes to steal, kill and destroy..." that is why they teach against getting rich. They are possessed with siding with the devil. But I am sent to tell you that poverty is a spirit. God did not mean for you to be poor. Come to think of it what does He gain in you being poor? The answer is nothing! God is into blessing you. The anointing upon you is a wealth magnet.

However, there needs to be a great balance on this wealth transfer revelation. There are those who will say we do not need to be wealthy for we cannot be wealthy and spiritual at the same time. On the other hand there are those who want to pile up car after car, then plane after plane but have nothing to do with the spreading of the gospel. They think they are following scripture by changing *"my cup runneth over"* to *"my garage runneth over with cars"*. That becomes selfish if God is not put first. That is the devil at work when one thinks nothing of giving to God's work whilst they increase in wealth.

Those who do not give to God are is simply a pack of gluttonous wolves masquerading as believers. They want to take over the wealth of the wicked for the wrong reasons. If you are one of these STOP reading this book. It is not for you! This is not one of those get rich quick schemes. It is a revelation for you to be a kingdom financier. See what happened during the time of Moses. People gave too much towards the work of God that Moses had to yell STOP! Exodus 36 vs. 6 says;

...Moses gave commandment... let neither man nor Woman make any more work for the offering of the Sanctuary. So the people were restrained from bringing.

The people were restrained because there was now an overflow in the house of God. There was now more than was needed! Money was no longer an issue. This is what should happen.

Notice; These things you are reading are not things I got excited about some short time ago and decided to teach you. This is not just a revelation. It's not just the word of God BUT a manifestation of the word of God I have seen to work over and over again. This is changing revelation to taking on a new way of life. It will be manifestation of a revelation of the word of God in action to you if you follow the principles too.

I have people that have heard this message from some of our resources and have been turned from poor to rich in a few months and a few that have changed their lives completely in a matter of days. Some have already started their work as money missionaries. They are being loaded with benefits as proclaimed in:

Psalm 68 vs.19
> **Blessed be the LORD, who daily LOADETH us with BENEFITS... SELAH.**

God wants you well and rich. He takes *"pleasure in the prosperity"* of His children. Because you have His backing, the lease the devil got from Adam is running out. The wealth of the wicked is now ours. It's not time for him to still own your workplace, your bank and the marketplace.

The time for the greatest wealth transfer is now!

If you have been rich and you have been poor at a certain stage in your life, you would agree with me - rich is better.

The Journey To Taking Over The Wealth Of The Wicked

However, the journey to taking over the wealth of the wicked starts by creating the mindset of wealth, BUT IN ORDER TO CREATE a right mental attitude towards wealth and all the other principles that are given here by the Holy Spirit - there is also a necessity to know the biggest prevention to wealth, which is that there is lack of revelation in the body of Christ concerning the right and wrong way of receiving wealth.

Since faith begins where the will of God is known - believers ought to know the will of God pertaining to the revelation of the right and the wrong way to receive. They ought to know the **'Lambano'** and the **'Dechomai'** of receiving wealth.

Chapter Two
The Two kinds of Receiving

When the Lord spoke to me in a vision at the beginning of 2007 and told me about the two kinds of receiving, I did not expect an explosion of miracles to happen any more than I expected to be the first person to land on the moon. That revelation ushered the God of the breakthrough right in to my house and into my life.

He said *"My people have not heard about the right or wrong way to receive what I have freely given them. They do not know that there is a right and a wrong way to receiving when it comes to wealth. So many of my people wait for things to fall on their lap and some keep on begging for what they already own and some have their hope in their spirits and faith in their mind which will never work"*

The Lord then enlightened me that though the believer is born into the right family, born in a place of wealth, born where the money was and still is – the believer lacks this knowledge of the two kinds of receiving, *'lambano'* and *'dechomai'*. He also **revealed to me that to any believer** armed with this revelation, attaining wealth should never be a struggle.

Many believers, because they lack this knowledge of *'lambano'* and *'dechomai'* are poor and beggarly because they expect the material riches and spiritual blessings promised in the word of God to just fall on them while they sleep, sing, pray or fast. Now when the Lord gave me that revelation and showed me the *right and wrong way of receiving wealth*, I began to realise what has been stopping many believers from making the wealth transfer a reality even though God had said the child of God was supposed to have God's best and was rich beyond their wildest imagination, way before they were even created.

Receiving the right and the wrong way

Notice just as one cannot use volleyball rules in a soccer match, one cannot also use a certain type of receiving where another kind of receiving is required. This is because there are two kinds of receiving that a believer has to understand in order to start operating in God's best concerning taking over the wealth of the wicked.

Now, I have been rich and I have been poor. Believe me, RICH is better!

Prosperity is the right of every believer. Receiving wealth, be it as a result of taking the wealth of the wicked or as a result of just acquiring wealth as written in *Matthew 19 v 29 and Mark 10 v 30* requires this revelation of how to receive the right way. As abovementioned, **what is not known** among believers today is the fact that there is a right and a wrong way to receiving the blessings God our father gave us.

Look at what the Lord showed me;

Matthew 19 v 29 and Mark 10 v 30:
> **And everyone who has left houses or brothers**
> **Or sisters or father or mother or wife or children**
> **Or lands, for my sake shall RECEIVE a hundredfold**
> **in this life.**

In receiving the hundredfold, the Lord Jesus Christ uses a particular *word* which describes the action of receiving; **'lambano'**. This word gives an idea of *taking, seizing as if by force*, actively taking and among other meanings it means *to seize so as to make use of* and with the end result *in point of fact* to putting into use what has been seized.

The word the Lord did not use in this particular verse is **'dechomai'** which also appears in our English scriptures as *receive*, like in the parable of the sower where it says:

Luke 8 v 13
> **They on the rock are they, which, when they hear,**
> **RECEIVE (dechomai) the word with joy; and these**
> **have no root...**

The translation of these two words into English as 'receive' has led so many believers to be ignorant of the revelation to be obtained in understanding these two kinds of receiving; *dechomai* and *lambano*.

Dechomai

Dechomai means to accept, welcome, receive subjectively, and receive what has been handed to one or given.

23

This word 'dechomai' unlike **lambano** denotes more or less a passive receiving that might not require an extended outward action. Dechomai will not work since this wealth is laid up for the believer and need believers to actually go and get. Believers need to go and get the wealth on their own and not simply dechomai – extend a hand. We as believers need to *wake up and smell the Money*, move into its direction and LAMBANO IT – take it as if by force!

Lambano wealth, DO NOT Dechomai!

In getting wealth, the Lord says in Matthew 19 v 29 and Mark 10 v 30 *seize as if by force the hundredfold riches and not just* dechomai - accept or welcome riches.

Whilst welcoming prosperity into one's heart is good there should be a taking or a seizing of wealth by *actively receiving* and through the pages of this book I will, by the Holy Spirit outline ways of how to **lambano** wealth, be it financial, spiritual or physical.

Now, let's say someone buys a brand new Mercedes, or if you are a Bentley fan lets use Bentley as an example. Then that person brings it to your house and gives you the keys which, if you are like me, you will accept the car. By accepting the car you will have 'dechomaid' the car. You simply accepted the gift. Once you start driving the car to work or just start using it generally, that is when you will have 'lambanoed' the car. You have taken in order to actively use and have actually *in point of fact* used the car. You see!

Notice the word says in Deuteronomy 8 vs. 18

It is He that gives you POWER to get rich...

It is Not the WEALTH but the POWER that God gave into our hands. We dechomai the power but we have to use the power we dechomaid from God and lambano riches with it. That means we need to activate that power on our own. Wealth is laid down and we need to go and use that power to take it in to our possession.

In my house, my wife has the keys to my most-valued Mercedes Benz. This version of Mercedes Benz has some technological gismos that need to be put into operation when driving the Mercedes. I have given my wife the power or right to use that

Mercedes and the password to operate everything in it. She has the password to the gismos – meaning she has the power to use the Mercedes and all the things in it. BUT, just because she has the password and the power to use the gismos and drive the Mercedes does not mean the password and that right drives the Mercedes. No it does not, for that is simply the first step. She needs to get in to the car and use the password in order to work things out, not just dechomai the password and the power to use the car. In order for the car to start moving she needs to drive it using her owns hands. The password does not drive the car and neither will the power or right she has to the car. She has to lambano!

My wife can drive – I taught her to do that too so it will be upsetting and on her part or stupid if I find her crying to me "my husband I need a password to the car and the power to drive it when she knows she has the right password and the authority to use that car. Many believers are like that, they are crying rivers to God till oceans flow asking for wealth when God has already given them power to get the riches. They have not realised that they have all the power they need to get rich and all that is left for them to do is **Lambano.**

You cannot be rich by believing you will be rich. Believing is a noun – Faith is a doing word. Faith is an ACTION WORD. Faith is a verb and a verb is an act. Believing is 'dechomai' and FAITH is' lambano'.

Notice, dechomai and lambano are two words that stand side by side just like receiving the Kingdom and entering the Kingdom. The Kingdom has to be received and entered or taken hence;

Matthew 11 vs.12
...the violent take it by force.

'Lambano' then has to come after one dechomais something. Many believers without realising have stayed on *dechomai,* believing that - that is all that is required of them. They sing songs, pray good prayers and fast often but still wonder why they are not getting the rewards promised by the word and some have gone to the extremes of rejecting the faith and prosperity part of the message as false all because they could not understand why they were not prospering. So it led them to believe that part of the message was not for them. They failed to **lambano.**

They have failed to know that rich people who are not in the kingdom work for their money and heap up wealth without knowing that they are doing this heaping up of riches for the believer. In short the rich people on earth are all working for the child of God AND believers have failed to see it. See it for yourself:

Ecclesiastes 2 vs.26
> **...to the sinner God giveth travail to GATHER and HEAP UP riches that he may give to him that is a believer Of God.**

That is why the Apostle Paul says

Romans 8 vs.28
> **...We know (eido - we are aware) all things work together for them that love God...**

This does not mean to say when bad things happen God is trying to teach the believer something. No, it does not mean that at all. See, believers have been brainwashed by the lies of the devil into blaming God. Romans 8 vs. 28 means all the people, all the companies, all the institutions of the unbelievers are working for my good. *They are heaping up riches that I am created to take (LAMBANO) and use for the kingdom of God*. The believer becomes rich because God has created workers that heap up riches for the believer. This might not sound fair to the unbeliever but unless one joins this train of Christ they are working for me and for every believer, come what may. Whether fair or not they will be working for us - the believers. Believers should work up and smell the MONEY. See:

Proverbs 13 vs.22
...the wealth of the wicked is stored up for the believer...

The above scripture starts by noting that **"a good man will leave an inheritance for his children's CHILDREN"** That is NOT a generational curse but a *generational blessing* and connects that to the part that declares **"wealth of the wicked**

is stored up for the believer" because the inheritance that the believer will leave for his children comes in part from the wealth the people on this earth have already worked for. So these people who are not in the kingdom are helping me leave an inheritance for my children if I happen to take over their wealth. If I only happen to *lambano*. *Boy, I love Jesus!*

Understanding the two kinds of receiving

Many times you hear people say being rich is not for everyone or getting healed is not for every Christian. This is not a surprise when one understands the two kinds of receiving. People who say these things expose the fact that they have not *lambanoed* their healing or wealth which is already purchased in full for them by the Lord Jesus Christ. Their denial to accept the message of taking over the wealth of the wicked is still a result of their failure to *lambano!*

Notice *lambano* and *dechomai* go hand in hand with believing and faith. They carry the same definitions and are easily confused. Many think that to *lambano* is to *dechomai* as much as they think to *believe* is to have *faith* and that is a lie the devil has used to keep believers poor for years. When one understands the difference between *believing* and *faith then they* have mastered the secret of taking over the wealth of the wicked.

Believing Is Not Faith

You cannot be rich by just believing that you will be rich. Believing is a noun – Faith is a doing word. Faith is a verb and a verb is an act. Believing is 'dechomai' and FAITH is' lambano'. You need to act upon that which you believe.

To believe is different to having faith. Just as a dog is not a cat and a cat not a dog. Believing is not faith and faith is not belief. However, belief and faith work together. Belief writes the digits on the cheque but it is faith that cashes the cheque. Though belief is the starting point of faith, it will not change the circumstances of your life. It is faith that changes your circumstance.

Faith is ACTING upon what you believe. Believing is done in the heart and ends there, yet faith is in the heart and is proven with an outward action. Without that action on the outside there is no faith. What will be present is *'believing'* and *believing* ends in the heart. It is not faith for it has no action attached to it. It ends in the heart. That explains why we have people that can talk of wealth and even believe it is God's will for them to be rich yet at the same time living a pauper's life. Believing is in the heart, only faith extends to the physical realm.

Romans 10 vs. 10
...with the heart man believeth...

When the believing is done in the heart you need to ACT UPON IT for it to be faith, otherwise it will simply be belief and that will not change your circumstance. See!
Believing is only the starting point and if all you do is believe in your heart but do nothing about what you believe then there will be no faith. In so saying – **dechomai** is of the heart and ends there but **lambano** comes out of the heart to perform in the natural what has been dechomaid or believed by the heart.

The example

Let me show you with an example. If you go into your kitchen and put a pot full of water on the stove and raise up your hands and say "I really believe that if I put the stove ON this water in the pot will boil". You will be there until you die unless you put your finger on the **'ON'** button for the water to boil. Though your believing might be very right, it will not make the water boil if the **'ON'** button needed to heat up the stove is not pressed.

You need to ACT UPON what you believe for it to work and that is great faith. That is the God kind of faith. THAT IS LAMBANO. See:

James 1 vs.22
...be doers of the word and not hearers only...

Believing that you will make money through selling cars is good BUT it will not make you any money until you actually put pen to paper, hand to work and buy used cars and really begin to sell used cars. Only then can you make money.
Believing you will make money is essential but really selling the

cars in the natural is lambano. *Lambano* is how God created the earth. He believed first and the acted upon that belief. After five days of creation, God made man in His likeness and crowned mankind with supernatural ability to do what He does.

2 Corinthians 5 vs.20
> **Now then we are ambassadors for Christ...**
> **Copying God's own lambano**

When God created the earth He needed to ACT upon what He had believed upon so as to bring things into existence. Again look at this;

Genesis 1 vs. 2
> **...the spirit of God MOVED upon the face of the deep...then God SAID...**

The word *moved* is *Rachaph* which means to *brood over in constant imagination of an outcome.* God thought of what the earth will be like before He created it. He fed the picture into Himself and then spoke it and acted like it was so before it came to be. That is to lambano. *Acting out what is in the inner man.*
Again When Jesus entered Capernaum and it was heard that He was in a certain house. Immediately many gathered together, so that there was no longer room to accommodate them, not even near the door as scripture tells us and He preached the word to them. Then came to Him four men with a paralytic friend. The Bible says;

Mark 2 vs.1-4
> **And again Jesus entered Capernaum after some days;**
> **and It was noised that He was in the house. And straightway many were gathered together,**
> **insomuch that there was no room to Receive them. And they come unto Him four men bringing unto Him one sick of the palsy. When they could not come nigh to Him because of the crowd, they uncovered the roof where He was and when they had broken it up, they let down the bed wherewith the sick of the palsy lay.**

These men had dechomaid that healing was with Jesus way before He came to their town. They had dechomaid that Jesus healed yet their receiving or their *dechomai* did not heal their friend. All their believing in Jesus' healing power did not heal their freind. They were lacking something. What they needed was to **lambano** the healing by really going to the Lord Jesus with their friend. They needed to put an **action** to what they believed. They need what was in them to be evident here in the natural not just in the heart. They needed to ACT UPON what was in their hearts. They needed what they had dechomaid to turn into *lambano*. They needed a physical proof of what they had on the inside. Look at how the Lord Jesus responded:

Mark 2 vs.5
When Jesus SAW their faith...

Now, how can faith be seen? Faith can be seen because it is an ACT. It is acting upon what you believe in. Mark 2 vs.1-10, the four friends BELIEVED that their friend was to be healed if they brought him to Jesus but they did not end there they ACTED upon that BELIEF and uncovered the roof to let down their friend and JESUS SAW THEIR FAITH. He saw them ACT upon what they believed. That is how believers should take over the wealth of the wicked. They ought to act out in the natural what they believe with the heart. And what they believe with the heart is that:

Ecclesiastes 2 vs.26
...to the sinner God giveth travail to GATHER and HEAP UP riches that he may give to him that is a believer Of God.

And that:

Proverbs 13 vs.22
A good man leaves an inheritance to his children's children

BUT how do wise men leave an inheritance for their children's children? The answer is in the same scripture - Through the wealth *of the wicked which is stored up for them* and to get this wealth they must dechomai without leaving out lambano. The wealth of the wicked has to be lambanoed not only dechomaid.

One needs to talk wealth, act wealthy if they want to be wealth. See. You need to package yourself with where you are going and confess this reality everyday of your life because **successful believers confess daily what poor believers confess occasionally.** *Take notes!*

Get your future to move into you before you move in to it and realise whilst doing this acting upon what you believe should be the concrete by which you take over the wealth of the wicked. Have your faith intact. Act upon what you believe. If you believe you will be a great business man then register a company and start trading in something.

Understand that even Jesus operated with these principles. You remember when His disciples came to him to tell him they had no swords? Did he say to them *"lets pray for them"* Did he say *"lets believe for them"* No He did not. He told them to go out and *do a little business*!

Luke 22 vs. 36
> **...He that has two pieces a coat let him sell
> One and buy a sword...**

To believe is only to have confidence in or to trust in but to act upon that confidence or trust is FAITH. Acting upon that confidence or trust is *lambano*.

How to lambano

Just as I have mentioned before, if you have a key to an automobile in your pocket you can believe that the key will start your car, and there will be nothing wrong with your belief. You can believe that the car will take you home, and your belief will be right. But it will never start the car or take you home until you put the key in the lock and turn it on. God's word is the key. You can believe His word is the key. But until you act on it and put it into the lock of life, into the circumstances of life, it will never do you any good.

"Whatever is not of faith is sin" (Romans 14:23) and God hates sin. When we don't believe God, we treat Him like He is a liar so when we do not lambano or act upon the word of God we are simply saying your word God is not true. When God says He has made us rich – we should start packaging ourselves with what He says. This is irregardless of whether I can prove it in the natural. All I need is to act upon what He says. If God says He has put His love in me – I have to start doing what love does even when I do not feel like it. You might ask 'is that not lying if I say what is true in the natural?' The answer will be, NO, That is not a lie because all I am doing is doing the truth according to the word of God and before you know it what I am told to do by God invades the physical realm. Notice what the word says:

2 Corinthians 4 vs.18
For we do not look at things that are seen for
The things that are seen are temporal.

The word temporal means subject to me changing the things that are seen. It paints a picture that everything I see can be changed. God's prerequisite is for the believer to simply act like those things that are troubling him/her have already been changed, and not to be affected by what happens in the seen realm. The act is not just spiritual but has to be a lambano. I need to act like things are already so, way before those things change in the natural. So I need to talk like I am already paid! Lack of faith leads to lack of obedience. God's commands can only really be fulfilled through acting upon what you believe which is really how to lambano. Without confidence in God's promises a man will never really lambano. They will never act like what God said needs to happen. Acting upon what God's word says is living by faith.

"The just shall live by faith" (Romans 1:17). We must live by faith for this is the only way we survive as believers.

Lambano a Miracle

When my son was born, he was born with *one kidney and the* doctors told us that they could not do anything about it. I never said anything back. Why? Because in my house we live by faith and doctors to me have never been the voice of God. God said to lambano so I said to my wife lets act like we know from the word that he has two kidneys. We agreed with God's word. Acted upon what we believed – we lambanoed and after many scans they could not believe what they were seeing when two kidneys where now showing on the screen. We lambanoed our son's kidney and he is well because of acting upon what we believed. Our son is alive and well because we lambanoed. We did not just dechomai, we also lambanoed. We did not just believe, we had to have faith.

Wealth Miracle

I am here to get you to possess wealth. I want every believer to own properties and have so much wealth that your enemies *will have hiccups* when they realise their new found wealth.

Wealth Miracles should be an everyday occurrence to every Christian who loves God. To every Christian money should never be an option.

Receiving the wealth of the wicked

It should be noted that *Dechomai* and *lambano* may overlap in meaning, however *dechomai* more frequently indicates a welcoming or an appropriating response where *lambano* which is used by Christ in the hundredfold blessing frequently speaks of a self prompted taking or seizing. It is to obtain by wrapping up or taking up. **It is a more active** possessing.

Let us look at Apostle Paul's use of *dechomai* in:

I Thessalonians 1 v 6
> **And you became followers of us, and of the Lord, having RECEIVED the word in much affliction...**

Here dechomai indicates a receiving of the word into the heart. Whereas lambano shows an outward participation of what is in the heart so as to bring what is inside to manifest on the outside. Notice all God's promises are:

2 Corinthians 1 vs. 20
> **...yea and in Him amen...**

This means that all the promises of God to us are all done deals but they have to be taken. They require an active participation of our will. God does not override our will so He leaves a part where we participate in the taking (lambano) what He has provided. See! *The Word dwells in you at the level by which you practice or* **lambano** *it.*

Don't just talk of starting a business...you need to start the physical process of starting a business. There is need to move confession to get into a confession to keep and increase upon that which you obtained through acting upon the confession to get.

Lambano is an active receiving that spills out to show an outward participation of what is inside. Dechomai is an inside receiving. No wonder the word of God says;

1 Corinthians 2 vs. 14
> **The natural man can not receive (dechomai)**
> **The things of the spirit...**

The natural man cannot accept the things of the spirit. Why? Because the things of the Spirit require those with a repentant spirit, a captivated spirit which can *'dechomai'* first before *lambano*. If one is to *lambano* God's truth first before *dechomai* they might keep what they have seized but then start to think the things of the Spirit are foolish and silly and therefore cannot be followed. If they only lambano without dechomai they will think they did it on their own when in fact it is all God's doing that gave them wealth. Lambano and dechomai all need to happen before the blessings of wealth or any other blessing can take place. See! Notice:

Acts 8 v 14-15
> **Now when the apostles which were at Jerusalem**
> **heard that Samaria had received (dechomai) the**
> **word of God, they sent Peter and John; who when**
> **they were come down, prayed for them that they**
> **might Receive (lambano) the Holy Ghost...**

The people received the word. They *dechomaid* the word but then Peter and John had to be sent over to them so they would know how to *lambano*.

There is a key word there - **MIGHT**. This shows that it was up to the people Peter and John prayed for to *lambano*. It was not a passive receiving. Don't you know the word says:

Psalm 68 vs.1
Let God arise...

It also says:

Ephesians 6 vs.16
...Taking up the shield of faith...

This shows that it is up to the believer to really take advantage of what God has given them. That is why one can believe God wants them to be rich but they will still be poor. That is why many who believe God wants them well and healed can remain sick. Revelation is not the truth you know. **Revelation is the truth you use**. Remember *the Word dwells in you at the level by which you practice or **lambano** it.*

Receiving an answer to prayer

One kind of receiving also needs to occur here for one to have a guarantee in getting prayers for wealth and for other things answered. This word is still *lambano* - to seize as if by some force. *Dechomai* is not found here but this does not mean it is not important. It is a starting point but *lambano* is the word that surfaces in the prayer of faith.

Matthew 21:22
And all things, whatsoever you shall ask in
Prayer, believing, you shall receive.

ALL THINGS, not *some* but ALL THINGS. Not only *all things* but WHATSOEVER we ask in the prayer of faith we should *lambano* - receive actively with an attitude of seizing as to make use of.

This use of *receive* is like the use of *believing* and *faith*. Though believing is good, it will not keep the boat afloat. Believing like dechomai (accepting) it will give you a good attitude and will even write a smile on your face whilst the ship is sinking. With dechomai only, *you will die with a good* attitude. *You will starve to death whilst smiling* but when you add *Lambano* to *dechomai* - you will be in faith. It is only when one acts upon what one believes that faith is produced and faith can keep the boat afloat. Likewise, dechomai will put a smile on your face but only lambano will bring the things you want into this physical world. Only **lambano** will usher the riches of the wicked into your hands.

Acting for answered prayer

At one time my wife and I were faced with financial concern over a meeting that we were supposed to hold within a few weeks from that point. Being people of faith and teachers of it, we decided to pray the prayer of faith. We glorified God, thanked Him for all the things that we were blessed to have and the provision of that money we didn't have. We started speaking as if we had the money.

As we started confessing that the meeting was going to go on despite the fact that we did not have the thousands needed to hire the hall, band and all the other necessities, we started acting upon what we believed. I called a few people discussing and confessing that the conference was going to go on without a problem. I kept muttering under my breath the revelation God had told me to preach for this event. My wife also went ahead with the arrangements for a meeting we did not have money for. Some minutes later, there was a knock on our door and a lady who attended our church came in and said; "Pastor, the Lord told me to give you this money". It was a wad of money with the bands from the bank still on it!

We had managed to dechomai (accept) in our hearts that God would provide but we also went on to *lambano by our confession and all our physical actions*. We wanted the money and it manifested in the natural.

See! We could have stopped at believing or accepting (dechomai) that God is a provider and would give us the money when the right time came, but that would be missing it. We had to act like what we believed was already so. We had to hold meetings with the ushers and the hotels that were to host the event as if all was well; we had to:

Romans 4 vs.17
...Calleth those things that are not as if They were...

We had to tell other people that the meeting was going on. I had to prepare to preach, pray for the sick and teach the people. My wife had to agree with me on the inside and also on the outside by planning and physically preparing for the conference. *Acting upon what one believes is the way to* **lambano** - seize as if by force but this only starts when one has first believed or accepted the fact that Jesus will provide the need - which is dechomai - accepting or welcoming something as fact. When you do, you get acquainted with God. Look at what God says when you accept Him;

Job 22 vs. 21
Acquaint now thyself with Him, and be at
Peace: thereby good (prosperity etc.) shall
Come unto thee.

The word also says;

2 Timothy 1 vs. 12
I am acquainted in whom I have believed

God speaks positive and acts positively so I acquaint myself with Him, with what He does and my following Him will yield results.

Everything has already been provided for; all I am waiting for is to bring those things from the spiritual realm to this natural realm or simply from another physical locale to my house. If I want a top of the range Mercedes bus to carry the people of God in, I will simply change the location of the bus from Germany to my house in England by faith Remember faith does not simply believe God but it acts upon the word of God.

When one understands this truth, miracles will become an everyday occurrence.

Everything has already been provided to the believer by the Holy Spirit. What is now left is for us to *lambano* - to take a hold of things mainly from the devil who has stolen them. We are not demanding from God but from the devil who is the thief.

Further explanation of dechomai and lambano
Dechomai mainly happens internally whereas lambano is a **'spiritually physical'** action.

In the will of God when people ask, things manifest but it is left to our free will whether to accept and take (dechomai and lambano) or accept and not take (dechomai) or simply not accept at all. Look at Luke 11 vs. 10 NKJ;

For every one who asks receives (lambano)
And he who seeks finds...

It is an action. In 1 John 5 vs. 15 we know we are guaranteed that when we pray according to His will, which is His word, we have an assurance that we have. So if we have this guarantee then what is left is to take a hold of what is around us. This is different from something falling on your lap. It should be an active reception. We read in

Mark 11 vs.24
>**Therefore I say to you, whatsoever things**
>**You ask believe that you (lambano) receive them**
>**And you will have them.**

Seen that!
You need to believe that you seize your request by an active stance and only then will you be guaranteed that you will have.

If we look at John 16 vs. 24 and 1 John 3 vs. 22 you will notice that the English translation will make it look as if there is nothing you really need to do except pray and be a good Christian for you to get answers to prayer. However that will be a grave miscalculation. Notice this verse of scripture;

John 16 vs. 24 NKJ
>**Until now you have asked nothing in my name,**
>**Ask and you will receive (lambano - seize as if**
>**By force) that your joy may be full**

Now, I want you to notice something. This does not mean to say it is a war to get the things that you want - it is simply a "good fight of faith".

What is a fight of faith?

It is my faith working against the lack of money,
It is my faith working against the symptoms of cancer or any

other disease in my body,
It is my faith working against an eviction order,
It is my faith working against my rocky marriage etc.

That is the fight of faith. You receive, you lambano and not station yourself on accepting only (dechomai). In order for wealth to come to the body of Christ for the furtherance of the Kingdom, we must lambano God's blessings. See,

1 John 3 vs. 22 NKJ
   And whatever we ask we receive (lambano)
   From Him, because we keep His commandments
   And do those things that are pleasing in His sight

Notice that in this verse of scripture we are told that we are able to seize the blessing, to *lambano* whatever we ask because we do what He commands since we are endowed with the supernatural ability to cause changes.

When we speak of lambano as an action-filled taking, we are not talking of some warfare somewhere or a ritual of some sort. This is a matter of faith. A fight of faith, acting upon what one believes. That is it!

Is lambano a war with the devil or a resting?

Some believers have overemphasised spiritual warfare to the extent that it goes out of line with the word of God. As a matter of fact many things that are taught in some churches today are simply scriptural errors and at most extremes that should be avoided. That is why I need you to understand that the use of *lambano* does not denote war but a resting in faith. No wonder Apostle Paul calls it the good fight of faith. A fight cannot be a good one unless one has already *won* before going into the ring.

A wrong mentality of warfare has led to a wrong believing and to accepting (dechomai) the wrong thing which in turn leads to some people 'lambanoing' the wrong things. It may surprise people if they are to know that never in the epistles where the words 'war' and 'warfare' used will one ever find the words Satan, Lucifer or devil used in connection with each other except when the armour of God was mentioned at the same time with the 'Evil one'. However there is an influence of the devil to everything that stands against God.

The warfare of a Christian is mainly;

2 Corinthians 10 vs.4-5
> **For the weapons of our warfare are not carnal,**
> **But mighty through God to the pulling down of**
> **Strongholds; casting down imaginations, and every**
> **High thing that exalteth itself against the knowledge**
> **Of God, and bringing into captivity every thought to**
> **The obedience of Christ...**

If you take the above verse in its context you will realise that to seize by force (lambano) is not a war as some have believed for so long. It is a way to fight a good fight. It is simply acting upon what one believes and that is faith in its purest form. The concept here is that 'When my bible says it, I have to believe it, and I have to act upon it and that settles it' When I have done the acting upon what I believe part, that means I will have succeeded in *lambanoing* and ready for the hundred fold blessing of God or the throtyfold or whatever fold he wants to give me.

Notice how Apostle Paul instructs Timothy;

1 Timothy 1 vs.18-19
> **This charge I commit unto thee, son Timothy,**
> **According to the prophecies which went on before**
> **Thee, that thou by them mightiest war a good**
> **WARFARE; Holding FAITH, and A GOOD**
> **CONSCIENCE;**
> **Which some having put away concerning faith have**
> **Made shipwreck:**

Did you see how Apostle Paul told Timothy to lambano or fight the good fight? He says to hold on to faith - that is acting upon what one believes and also to keep a good conscience. This is what we call resting not at war. Believers should understand the generic language of scripture and the language of Paul to be exact.

Guaranteed answers to prayer will come when we pray God's will and act upon it. This guarantee does not stay with God, He already guaranteed us in 1 John 5 vs. 15 as was seen before. Now what we need to do is accept it (dechomai) and then seize (lambano) the answer with the intention of not letting go. That's to lambano. To keep a good conscience, to cast down imagination, bring every thought into captivity to Christ and act upon what we believe. That is to *lambano* for answered prayer. It gives a guarantee for prayer to be answered.

Short circuiting the power to lambano

In this issue of lambanoing is a great number of people leaving churches to follow so called men and women of God who look like they have it altogether and seem to have lambanoed the wealth of the wicked and some already have. In the same group are preachers that just want a good crowd. These Preachers who have run into this error might be sincere but they are sincerely wrong.

They do not rebuke people just as long as they have a huge crowd. They steal sheep from good Bible believing churches and feel they are growing and boast it is God doing it. No matter how flamboyant the man or woman looks or sounds if they steal sheep (people) from other good churches and do not rebuke people who have done wrong, they are simply;

Matthew 15 vs.14
...the blind leading the blind...

The sheep themselves are blind - they do not realise that what they want in the man they are following is exactly what others who are as blind as they are have given to the man. But the Bible says:

Proverbs 22 vs.16
Those who give to the rich shall surely be poor...

They want the flamboyance of the man, the riches he says he got from God but what they do not know is their offerings and tithes are exactly what is making the man drive the best cars, own properties and media stations, jets etc. If they were grown up in the Lord they would know that if they bind anything concerning their finances on their own, they will get what God being alpha and omega has already bound in Heaven.

The devil is at work yet many believers are too blind to notice. Many have left churches that God planted them in for a lousy dime. They do not realise that God cannot release to them His best because they run into disobedience by leaving where God has planted them. When they try to lambano it will not work because lambano works on obedience.

Back to You and the plunder

Now, concerning the Israelites' plundering of the Egyptians, we recognize that they were where God had said they will be and the alpha and the omega; the one that sees the end before making the beginning had already spoken in Exodus 3:22 saying, *"Your descendants will be strangers in a land that is not theirs, and will serve them, and they will afflict them four hundred years. And also the nation (Egypt) whom they serve I will judge;* **afterward they shall come out with great possessions***"* (Genesis 15:13-14, emphasis added). So when they were taking wealth it was simply a *lambano* of what God had prepared before hand making it easy to *seize by force.*

God gives us an opportunity to exercise faith and trust in the great I AM that wealth comes and wealth stays when we *lambano* with a wealth mindset that says God does it and not us. That is why we have to know that *lambano* is not warfare.

However this *lambano* can also be stopped if the believer who should live by faith starts living by the senses for the mind if not renewed by the word of God can hinder the receiving of the wealth of the wicked.

Senses vs. Receiving

If the devil keeps you in the sense realm, he will destroy your plans but if you keep him on the faith (acting upon what God says - lambano) side, you will walk in the victory the Lord gave us over the devil and be able to take up (lambano) His blessings.

Now, it is very easy to rely on sensory perception when it comes to wealth and many in the church today live that way although they may deny it.

Senses

Let's say you are to go through an operation to remove a growth in your stomach. The doctors will give you an appointment to attend surgery. When you do, they take you into the theatre where there will be doctors wearing masks, holding knives, pairs of scissors, laser pipes and many other tools. You are then laid back; you try to relax as you wait for the defining moment. Back on the street if you were to see a person with these same masks, scissors and above all knives, you would run. Yet in your complete trust you give consent to be operated on.

What normally happens is that you do not even ask to see the doctors' qualifications or even to see their faces. Remember they will be wearing masks let alone holding dangerous weapons. Asking them for proof that they are indeed real doctors never occurs to many because the senses are sure beyond depth and beyond height that they are really doctors and not murderers even though you don't have proof for it.

This blind trust you give your doctors is not at all bad sometimes but the same should also be used with regards to the things of the Lord God Almighty. The same trust you give your doctors should also be given to your God, even more. When He says it, you have to believe it, act upon it and that should settle every argument. This should be irregardless of what the physical evidence shows you.

In order to receive (lambano) the blessings of God, one has to understand that there is also a need to "cast down imaginations" as Apostle Paul says it. Senses have to be out of the way for faith to start manifesting. Senses have to be out of the way for lambano to start manifesting.

Scripture says;

2 Corinthians 4 vs. 18
> **While we look not at things that are seen but at the things that are not seen: for the things which are seen are temporary...**

Receiving (lambano) has to forget all the physical evidence that are against what God has said for **we walk by faith, not by sight (2 Corinthians 5 vs. 7)**

Wealth With A Mission!

When faith supersedes senses then money can be lambanoed or obtained with the main focus of furthering the Gospel. This wealth issue should never be our focus. Its purpose is the focus and should always be. Wealth should be wealth with a purpose if we are serious about getting the wealth of the wicked. The Lord Jesus Christ should be the real focus of obtaining wealth Money should be there to finance the spread of the gospel of Jesus Christ because if Jesus disappears from our focus the devil takes centre stage and poverty comes to us like a thief. So in taking over the wealth of the wicked receiving is important but after knowing the two kinds of receiving that wealth, believers ought to have the mindset of wealth since money goes to where it is understood!

Chapter Three
The Mindset of Wealth

There is nothing called an impossible situation; there are only impossible people in a situation. Taking over the wealth of the wicked becomes impossible when you think it's impossible but when you can think its possible then you will become a wealth magnet. You will start pulling resources to yourself. If you can think its possible to take over the wealth of the wicked, you will have transformed yourself into a magnate of resources. You will start pulling resources and riches to yourself. If fact resources willstart congregating around you. Notice what the word says;

Proverbs 23 vs.7
As a man thinks in his heart so is he...

See! If you can think it up, you can bring it down. If you think poor, you will believe poor, act upon being poor and ultimately become poor. But if you think big you will believe big and obtain big results.

If you can not think it, you can't get it.

Those who think big are not limited! Jesus never thought of Himself as poor. Remember what He said when Judas complained that it was better if the perfume that was put on Jesus was given to the poor? Jesus heard him and said;

Mark 14 vs.7
You will always have the poor but you will
Not have me...

He could have said I am also poor but He did not. What He said indicates His mind. It indicates what He thought and how He saw Himself.

Jesus thinks BIG!

Think of Jesus instructing His disciples to preach the gospel to every creature and to do it in every nation. This instruction was financially, physically, emotionally and numerically impossible. They were only twelve. They had no ships, planes and no way to

45

go. They had no money to carry out a mission of this enormous scale. It was also legally impossible. The law forbade them to speak in the name of Jesus or even mention the name of Jesus. It was socially impossible, for not many wanted to listen, yet Jesus thought big. Circumstances did not limit Him. He knew that if He could think big, He could believe big, act upon that which is big and get big results and He got it. That is why you are holding this book and that is why I am teaching these principles. We are all believers as a result of Jesus thinking big.

Mark 16 v 15 says;
> **Go ye into all the world and preach the gospel...**

The Lord thought big, believed big, commanded big, expected big and got big results. If you can only think big you can bring it down. Apostle Paul says;

Philippians 4 vs. 8
> **Whatever is good, whatever is profitable THINK On these things...**

Creating the mindset of wealth requires thinking on the purpose of wealth. Many who preach on wealth have lost the plot by not informing their listeners on the purpose of wealth. Wealth is for financing our lives so that we can have enough to finance the kingdom. Wealth is supposed to be used for the work of God. The fulfilment of the spreading of the gospel to the untold requires those who think big, dream big, willing and obedient. It requires a creation of the mind that is wealth compliant for money goes to where it is understood.

You can not *think poor and expect to be rich*. You can't think weak and expect to be strong. You can not think *'servant'* and expect to an employer. It is impossible. Everything starts with how you think a thing up. It all starts with replacing 'impossibility' thinking with 'possibility' thinking. Remember the Lord Jesus says in

Mark 9 vs. 23
> **Anything is possible to him that believes...**

Possibility Thinking

Henry Ford who invented the v-8 engine thought of it as a possible thing to create it but his employees could not think it possible to build an entire engine with the entire eight cylinders placed in one block. Henry Ford's employees had no 'possibility' thinking. All they had was 'impossibility' thinking.

The engineers came to Ford and made it clear to him that it was IMPOSSIBLE to cast an eight cylinder gasoline engine block in one piece. When Henry Ford heard this he said "produce it anyway". He could not agree with the impossibility thinking patterns of his engineers.

"Sir, it is impossible to create it" they replied, yet Ford commanded them to get on with the job until they succeeded no matter how much time was required. Against their opinions they went to work anyway as Henry Ford had commanded. Where the engineers thought impossible, Ford thought big and possible.

After six months the engineers had not succeeded and to them it only proved that they were right all along. Ford seeing that this feat was seemingly impossible did not change his thinking. He kept thinking big and possible. At the end of the year, the situation was the same yet Ford kept his possibility thinking.

The engineers reminded him of what they had said about the job being an impossible task. "Keep working", Ford said. "I want it and I will have it". What transpired next made the Ford v-8 engine the most spectacularly successful car on the road and brought Ford to the forefront. He made the engine work all because of his possibility thinking.

Agree with God and the impossible will become possible
The wealth of the wicked can only be gathered by those who think big, believe big and act upon that which is big. Your mind should be filled with wealth with a mission. A mission to spread the word of God even to the far ends of the world... when we think big we are agreeing with God. Job 22 vs. 21 R.S.V. says;

Agree with God and be at peace; thereby
Good will come to you...

Good comes to you when you think big. God thinks big. The power of possibility thinking which the Lord Jesus used and which the disciples of Jesus used is available to us ward who believe. It is ours so we can take the wealth of the wicked which is already stored up waiting for us to take. Let us take a look at that scripture again;

Proverbs 13 vs.22
The wealth of the wicked is stored up
For the just...

We should concentrate on the purpose of wealth. It is alright to be rich, God wants you rich but it is wrong not to know why God wants you rich. See, all churches that do not take care of their pastor and their church are broke. The church will be broke and the members will be broke. Think God's work and He will think of your work and help you. If you think big and take care of God's business, God will take care of yours. He will open the eyes of your faith to help you take over the wealth of the wicked.

The wealth of the wicked belongs to us but for us to be able to make the biggest transfer of wealth the earth has ever seen WE SHOULD KNOW THE REASON WHY God wants us to take the wealth of the wicked. We should also believe that He wants us rich and to be able to believe it we should think it. Our thinking has to catapult us into greater heights in this area of taking over the wealth of the wicked.

Why we need to think first

Genesis 1vs.26 tells us that:
God made man in His image and likeness...

We were made in God's likeness so we could FUNCTION LIKE GOD!

Notice; cats give birth to cats, dogs to dogs, donkeys to donkeys and God to His own sons and daughters who look like Him and function like Him. Apostle Paul says;

Ephesians 5 vs. 1
Be ye therefore followers (imitators) of God
as dear children.

So we imitate God. If God thinks big before creating, then we think big before we bring things into manifestation. Do not fear to act like your father God because FEAR TOLERATED IS FAITH CONTAMINATED. God said to imitate Him so we think big just like He thinks big and we will get big results. Remember if you can think it up, you can bring it down. If you think poor, you will believe poor, act upon being poor and ultimately become poor. But if you think big you will believe big and obtain big results.

God thought So we think first and get the same results

Before God made the world he thought first! Notice carefully how He did it. You will be amazed at the power and when you master it you will have made steps in your path to taking over the wealth of the wicked.

To understand how we can have what we say we have to first understand how God does it and since we are imitators of God, we will also get what He gets when He thinks big. It is so easy to understand. This is not robotics...it is simply following what God says!

Faith begins where the will of God is known

In order to call those things that are not as if they were, you need to know the will of God with regards to your desires. See! *Faith always begins* where the *will of God* is known. Where the will of God is not known there can never be faith.

The will of God is easy to know -it is his word, the BIBLE- read it and you will know God's will for your life. After knowing His will, brood over that will in your spirit, imagine the outcome in your spirit, speak it out and then act as if what you are believing for and have spoken out is already so. That is how God did it and does it. This is the God way of doing things. This is exactly what he did in Genesis. Papa God Himself put this in to us who really believe in Him and are born again so we can follow His example.

Notice here in **Genesis 1 vs.1**
> **In the beginning God created the heavens**
> **And the earth.**

Contrary to what many have been taught, Genesis 1 vs. 1-2 happens only in the heart of God - it is a spiritual reality which is

49

absolutely limited to the spiritual and not evident physically. This is why verse 3 says "And God said let there be..." The word 'And' is also rendered "Then" so the verse says:

**In the beginning God imagined the heavens
And the earth...then he said let there be...**

This shows a clear follow up of events; God first imagines it just like the word 'created' rendered RACHAPH in the Hebrew in Genesis 1 vs. 2 means or in other words God produced it and restricted it to the spiritual realm, brooded over the idea in constant imagination of the physical outcome, THEN He SAYS "Let there be..." God called by His mouth those things that did not exist as if they were and the things obeyed by becoming existent, in the spiritual realm first and as chapter 2 shows, went on to bring it out in the physical. That is the reason you read in:

Chapter 2 verses 4-5 of Genesis
4. These are the generations of the heavens...
**5. Before every plant was in the field and before
Every herb in the field grew - for God had not
sent rain to water it and no man to till the soil.**

DO YOU see that? In Chapter 1 God is seen creating the earth, the plants, herbs and so forth, BUT all of a sudden the bible says in chapter 2 that the herbs and the trees which *we thought* were already physically there - were actually not physically evident because there was no man to till the ground. The vegetation was created on the third day and Adam was created in the 6th day. Do you see it? The third day vegetation was only a spiritual reality for God proves after creating man that the vegetation did not come into being on the third day like people think because there was no Adam or Eve to till the land. Here is *where the revelation is*.

The revelation being that God made the physical out of the spiritual, the seen out of the unseen and the possible out of the impossible by first brooding over the idea or simply creating it in the spirit, secondly by constantly imagining the outcome, thirdly by acting as if the things were already in the physical and then...BANG! It came to the physical. So here are the steps:

1. *Read God's word first, that is the will of God*, see if what you want is covered by the word of God - If wealth is covered in the word and it is then you have proof that if you want it you will get it.

2. *Brood over it* - think of the outcome and its impact – see yourself rich. See yourself RICH. Let the life of the wealthy move in to you before you move in to it!

3. *Act as if the thing you are hoping for is already so*- because it is in the spiritual the moment you decree it, but not yet so in the physical – keep thanking God for the wealth which you have received for in prayer though it is not yet evident in the physical.

4. Whilst doing step 1, 2 and 3 you should be busy walking in the light of your confession and thanking God for bringing it into existence and *it will manifest in the physical realm.*

Notice, you need to get God's will for your life first then imagine the outcome of that desire, the impact it will have, how it will help in furthering of the Gospel of the Kingdom of God, brood over it, act as if it is already so, then thank God for it and it will come into existence. God never said '*Wait until I give you what to decree first before you decree a thing.*' No He did not because His word already gives you what to decree. He simply said:

...You shall decree a thing and it shall be established...

You do it. You, you, you, and not God. *The only thing is you should have that thing in the word of God first for you to decree it. It should be covered by the word of God first. Look at this thing again.* Look at whatis said in"

Genesis 2 vs.3
> **God rested in the seventh day from all his**
> **Work which God CREATED AND MADE.**

See! First God CREATED or imagined in constant imagination of an outcome (rachaph) and then after that He MADE things exist from what He had already imagined.

Your Imaginative ability is your creative power

Let me prove it to you by the bible! 'CREATED' and 'MADE' as you see in Genesis 2 vs. 3 are two different words with completely different meanings. The Holy Spirit Himself placed these words to help you understand your imaginative ability. You imagine it then make it. Only man has got imaginative/creative ability.

When you look at Genesis 2 vs. 7 you will see that man was CREATED first then God FORMED him from the dust. See! Man was not created from dust; he was FORMED from the dust after God imagined him and brooded over it. This imaginative ability is what the word calls 'CREATING'. So God imagined and then spoke things into existence. In bringing man into existence, God created the earth, spoke it into existence and then formed man out of the earth He had brought into existence through saying or simply speaking it out. Note:

Genesis 2vs.7
   ...and the Lord God FORMED man of the DUST of the ground.

God did not CREATE man from the DUST, He FORMED man from the DUST. The word 'form' is the word which means "making from previously existing material". What was previously existing material? The EARTH, the ground! See, God Himself is releasing a revelation on how to understand taking over the wealth of the wicked. Start with understanding the will of God then birth a desire in your spirit, brood over the desire, imagine the outcome, act as if its already in the physical and then it will come. While doing these things keep saying *'I have it now'*.

Beware of thieves but don't dwell on them

There are those that will copy or imitate true men of God and then prophesy money out of your pocket but be warned - They have their reward already. Anyone who prophesies or preaches money out of your pocket is stealing from you. This wealth transfer does not mean lining the preacher's pockets. It is to enlarge the spreading of the word of the Kingdom. However in all my Christian life, I have noticed one thing; churches that pay their pastors well are rich. Even the congregants in those churches are rich. Those that do not think about their pastor's income are poor and continue to be poor. See, when the preacher is robbed of his pay by not paying him or paying him well, the people rob themselves of their ability to be blessed financially and every other way.

Now, some will label those who will dare preach this part of the message of Christ as heretic but as Apostle Paul said;

Acts 20 vs.24
None of these things move me...

I am not moved by criticism. I have received my share and will continue to receive more as I grow in my ministry and as dedicated saints continue to gather around our ministry. All men of God have suffered and some continue to be persecuted in the form of criticism and false accusations. If they did it to my Lord Jesus Christ, the same will happen to me.

Not being moved

I remember well the time I started moving in the prophetic ministry evidently. I would call out names of places I had never been to, names I had never heard of and of people I have never seen before. People started a rumour that I went to a certain African country to buy black magic (popularly known as 'juju'). Some people said it was a rare black magic potion that only a few can find and I, for some reason best known to them, happened to know the person who sells it to a chosen few.

Some said I was very good at guessing names and even the future. Others went to the extremes of saying I used to live in London in a certain posh place and whilst there I acquired some money to buy a so called 'magic portion' that makes people fall under the power. They said this particular 'magic portion' was always hidden in my suit jacket before each sermon. When I would remove my jacket whilst preaching and people continued to fall without anyone touching them the accusations changed to that my magic now had increased in power that I no longer needed to touch people or wear a magic portion. Some also fantasised that I interviewed the people before I gave out the prophetic words and with success I would bribe them into coming to my meetings and then pay them a hefty amount to accept as true all these names I was mentioning to them.

The latter accusations, however, seemed to have been made by very thoughtless people even by worldly standards since they could not address how I got with absolute accuracy dates of when earthquakes, disasters, deaths of personalities around the world like the death of the president of Papa New Guinea which I mentioned with accuracy three weeks before the event under the anointing and many other events and when news that affected the nations, the world or individuals would happen. Many times God has shown me dates when people would die, events in the world, floods, earthquakes, many natural disasters and I mentioned these things on camera way before they happened. The question to a 'wise' person will be "did I interview the earthquakes as well, did I use the so called 'magic potion' to predict the death of people or even head of states or maybe I phoned the president of Papa New Guinea and told him to die when he did?"

When my wife was informed of these accusations from a person we were witnessing to she simply said there was no black magic and in fact told the person we have never been to the country that those people were talking about, neither had we ever lived in London. After these accusations I was invited to the same country for a conference and I gladly went. As for the other unexplainable events that God showed me, my wife simply responded *"Maybe the Pastor interviewed the earthquakes and bribed the floods to happen before they happened, when they happened and after they happened and he must have told them where and when to happen as well and also tell the presidents and head of states to die when they did and where they did".*

See people will talk and try to rob you of your blessing and if you listen to every criticism and accusation you hear that is when the anointing lifts. An 'ichabod' will happen to you.

If you know God sent you to do what you are doing do not let any person distract you. God will never leave you nor forsake you. I have seen people leave good churches because of a single rumour but God has replaced them with better ones, especially in my ministry. One person leaves, God adds five more – that is what God specialises in. He will never leave you. If you ever want to take over the wealth of the wicked you have to get to grips with this truth...that those who leave you are seldom tied to your prosperity!

Just preach the real word no matter it's not popular and do not respond to critics. When you preach on taking the wealth of the wicked or simply believe it people will arm themselves with criticism against you. Rumour will be spun.

Do not respond to accusations.

However, soon after we responded to this, the Lord came and spoke to me about not responding to accusations at all. He said this ministry was not ours, it was His. So responding to people was an error, for by so doing we would be trying to keep our reputation and not God's reputation, for even His son was accused of using magic, of being Beelzebub, some even said He was simply a carpenter's son not capable or fit for what He was claiming to be. He also reminded me that in Nazareth His son was not received and that short circuited the power of God. I asked Him for the solution and He said to us:

"None of these things should move you. Persecution is simply the expression of Satan's fear." So nothing moves us and nothing should move you if you want wealth to come to you!

Those who oppose the fact that believers ought to be powerful in spirit, perform miracles as well as drive the best cars, live in the best houses, control the economies of the world and live posh here on earth have lost the plot. They cannot understand our level because they are at the back of our plane, they are back biters. These reprobate people do not understand some parts of the gospel. In the gospel there are spiritual blessings and there are also physical blessings. All these back biters accept and deal with are a few and not all the spiritual blessings and I teach all and that is true salvation (sozo) meaning whole- nothing missing, nothing broken just like the word shalom means.

Spiritual blessings guarantee physical blessings!

Now it's not your portion to concentrate on those who oppose you for they are worse than the demons of hell. Remember what Christ said;

Matthew 12 vs. 26
If Satan casts out Satan how will his kingdom Stand...

See! The devil is many times clever. He knows enough not to cast himself out. In fact the Lord said of him;

Matthew 12 vs. 43-45
When a spirit leaves a man... it looks for seven More stronger than he...

You see, the devil goes and gets other demons and all of them come back and enter the body that one of them was cast out of. Preachers now are fighting preachers. Christians are fighting Christians, yet demons don't! This makes those who criticise worse than the devil and his cohorts!

'Prosperity Gospel'
You have to sought it out in your mind that there is definitely nothing called "prosperity gospel", there is the gospel of Christ and that gospel of Christ as seen clearly in the word includes prosperity. I am not a prosperity preacher but *simply a preacher who happens to be prospering*. My calling is that of a Prophet. I am in the discerning of spirits, word of knowledge, Miracles and healing - I am send to teach the word and so here I am not talking about spiritual blessings only BUT physical; cars, houses, planes e.t.c. The spiritual will get you to the physical if you accept all the parts of the gospel. When the Bible says;

Genesis 13 vs.2
And Abram was very rich in cattle, in silver, and in gold...

The Bible is not talking about spiritual **cattle, silver and gold.** No the Bible is not talking about spiritual things here. These riches of Abraham are physical. There is nothing called spiritual cattle, spiritual silver or gold. **It is all about money!**

Thank God for those who preach healing. Thank God for those who concentrate on redemption in the spirit and thank God for those who were sent to awaken the body of Christ on the issue of wealth and for people like me who are sent to preach the WHOLE GOSPEL OF Jesus Christ with prophetic insight!

We the sons and daughters of God should, without regret have His best! *We should not be broke.* Not having money is not our portion in Christ. The wealth of the wicked is ours and it's high time you stop living from paycheque to paycheque no matter what the economic situation is in your country. Believers should be calling the shots wherever they go!

The devil uses money to control believers. Look, every time a country imposes or implements a policy that is against the United Nations, the U.N will impose economic sanctions on the country all because it is on money that Satan has a hold on in this world. So the moment we take over Satan's stronghold, he becomes limited.

The Devil also uses wealth for his work

Just look at how he tempted the Lord. Satan tempted the Lord with food and power; all in the physical. That was his hold. How did he get that? He got it from the fallen man Adam but the bible tells us that Jesus is the second Adam so we are taking it back and the moment we take a hold of that money and start calling the shots, we will limit his ammunition.

However, this is for those who do not focus on wealth but on its purpose. Those who will put their focus on wealth and not on its purpose are in for a surprise;

Proverbs 23 vs. 5
> **When wealth increases do not set your eyes**
> **On it... for surely it makes wings...**

Think God, think on wealth's purpose in the furtherance of the Holy Spirit, act upon wealth and you will have started on the road to getting the wealth of the wicked.

Rich does not mean Holy!

If you see a wealthy person, do not think in your mind that they are holy just because they are wealthy. Wealth is not the measurement of how holy a person is and *neither is poverty a lack of holiness.* Wealth is the will of God for us His children but should never be used to measure holiness. If it did then Warren

Buffet would be claiming to be the fourth member of the 'trinity', Bill Gates would be claiming to be a chief Apostle and Donald Trump would be claiming to be an Evangelist in this world. See!

Wealth does not measure holiness or lack of it. Wealth has a purpose and thinking wealth will help us on our journey to taking over the wealth of the wicked, so we can spread the gospel with it.

The mind of wealth

If your thoughts on wealth are wrong, you will make decisions to protect your feelings and not your future. Your spirit becomes overrun by your flesh, *you think poor; you will believe poor, act upon being poor and become poor!*

Your thoughts will affect how you feel and when 'how you feel' is affected, you will start acting upon your feelings in the flesh and oppose your faith. But if you think getting rich in the mind and agree with your spirit, you will believe rich, act upon that which is rich and ultimately become wealthy for a reason!

Your thinking will affect your attitude. The higher you go and how wealthy you become is as a result of how big you think. Remember what the word says;

Proverbs 23 vs.7
As a man thinketh in his heart so is he...

Whatever you think is what you will become. Think taking over the wealth of the wicked and you will have started on your way to getting the wealth of the wicked. We are not the poor sons and daughters of God trying to get rich. We are billionaires waiting to happen! We are the rich bringing out the riches into manifestation!

Negative thinking will produce negative emotions; negative emotions will give birth to negative decisions, negative decisions in turn produce negative actions, negative actions will produce a negative character and a negative character will produce a negative manifestation!

If you don't want to be poor change your negative thoughts with regards to taking over the wealth of the wicked, after that change your habit. In order to change your habit you need to change your actions and in order to change your negative actions, change your negative decisions and negative emotions. And for you to be able to change your negative emotions and all other negatives, change your NEGATIVE THINKING.

The higher you think, the wealthier you become for:

Proverbs 23 vs.7
As a man thinks in his heart so is he...

Thinking right attracts wealth. Wealth is attracted to those who understand wealth.
As men say, a fool and his money are easily parted.

Money goes **where it is understood.** When one *understands wealth,* miracle wealth answers the door. When one thinks of taking over the wealth of the wicked...the wealth of the wicked comes knocking. Miracle money will start pouring in. The plundering of the sinner will become the order of the day!

Miracle wealth

Now, are we talking of stealing from the ungodly here? Did God steal from the Egyptians and what is this miracle wealth or miracle money where people are just compelled to give their wealth to you? How could the Egyptians just hand over gold, silver and clothes to their slaves and how could God allow such thievery?

Many scriptures teach us that God can not break His own word yet in the case of the Egyptians God allowed something that looked like a big and unholy heist. We know that the word says in;

Psalm 138 v.2 says God has;
...exalted His name above all names and His word above His own name...

This means that the word of God is a law unto God. He can not break it. God follows His word. God is His word. He can not go back on His word. He cannot break it. *However, in the plundering of the Egyptians it seems as if he did just that. Why?*

Exodus 20 v 15 says
...thou shall not steal...

In the book of Leviticus God went on to say that "...you shall not steal, nor deal falsely...you shall not cheat your neighbour".

Do not cheat your neighbour? This seems to be exactly what the Israelites did at the command of God. They asked for gold, silver, clothes and the things they required and never returned the goods. Was this not stealing and wasn't God guilty of what other reprobate minds would call a 'holy heist'?

Apostle Paul also said thieves would not enter the Kingdom of Heaven and he also said under the unction of the Holy Spirit that "let him that stole steal no more". So how can God justify this?

Does God allow us to steal from the wicked?
If a thief was found breaking into a house and was struck so that he died, the Old Testament Laws which God put in operation stated that there would be

Exodus 22:2
No guilt for his bloodshed...

In fact, one of the Ten Commandments that God gave to Israel was:

Exodus 20:15
You shall not steal.

In the book of Leviticus, one can read where;

Leviticus 19:1-2, 11, 13
The Lord spoke to Moses, saying, 'Speak to all
The congregation of the children of Israel, and
Say to them... You shall not steal, nor deal falsely,
Nor lie to one another.... You shall not cheat your
Neighbour, nor rob him.

Under the new covenant, the apostle Paul wrote to the church at Ephesus, saying:

Ephesians 4:28
> **Let him who stole steal no longer, but rather**
> **Let him labour, working with his hands what is good,**
> **That he may have something to give him who Has need.**

And to the Christians at Corinth, Paul wrote that **thieves**;

1 Corinthians 6:10-11.
> **...Will not inherit the kingdom of God...**

Thus, God obviously considers stealing to be a transgression of His law. He considers it evil. Why then will he allow the Israelites to break the law which He Himself put in place and which He being the faithful God can not break?

Foolish minds, however, question the consistency of the above Bible verses when compared to other passages of scripture, which they feel often are overlooked in a discussion on the biblical view of thievery.

When God spoke to Moses at the burning bush about the Exodus from Egypt, He said:

Exodus 3:21-22, emphasis added
> **It shall be, when you go, that you shall**
> **not go empty-handed. But every woman**
> **shall ask of her neighbour, namely, of her**
> **who dwells near her house, articles of silver,**
> **Articles of gold, and clothing; and you shall**
> **Put them on your sons and on your daughters.**
> **So you shall plunder the Egyptians.**

When the Exodus became a reality, the Bible tells how,

Exodus 12:35-36, emphasis added
> **the children of Israel had done according to**
> **the word of Moses...and plundered the Egyptians**

It seems to some here that God tells the Hebrew women to break the eighth commandment by encouraging the Israelites to steal from the Egyptians. Some see Our Lord Jesus Christ as a great and smooth thief who stole donkeys.

Now, did Jesus really encourage His disciples to **steal** a donkey and a colt? And what about the Israelites plundering the Egyptians? Can these passages be explained logically in light of the numerous statements throughout Scripture that clearly condemn this kind of behaviour? Can we have a revelation from the word or an understanding from it that justifies or explains The Lord Jesus' behaviour.

A proper plundering OR an unholy heist?

The kind of plundering done by the Israelites is described within the text. God told Moses, "I will give this people (the Israelites) **favour** in the sight of the Egyptians.... But every woman shall **ask** of her neighbour, namely, of her who dwells near her house, articles of silver, articles of gold, and clothing; and you shall put them on your sons and on your daughters" (Exodus 3:21-22). When it finally came time for the Exodus, the text states:

Exodus 12:35-36, (emp. Added)
> **...asked from the Egyptians articles of silver, articles of gold, and clothing. And the Lord gave the people favour in the sight of the Egyptians, so that they granted them what they requested. Thus they plundered the Egyptians**

The actual meaning of borrowed is requested. This carries no intention of bringing back the goods. That is to mean the Egyptians knew their request was to take the goods forever and not to return them to the Egyptians. There is also a word that many forget in that verse and that word is FAVOUR as given in the verse above. The Israelites where given an uncommon favour that God has also placed upon us, so that when they asked they were given. Remember:

Matthew 7 vs.7
> **Ask, and it shall be given you; seek, and ye shall find; knock, and it shall be opened unto you: For every one that asketh receiveth; and he that seeketh findeth; and to him that knocketh it shall be opened**

The Israelites merely **requested** various articles, which were then granted by the Egyptians. The "plundering" described in the book of Exodus was nothing more than receiving that for which the Israelites asked and got because of supernatural favour.

What is plundering then and how do we plunder?

The word "plundered" in these two passages is not the normal Hebrew term used for what soldiers do to the enemy at the conclusion of a battle. In Exodus, the word "plundered" is from the Hebrew word *natsal* which is used figuratively to mean that the Israelites accomplished the same thing as if they had taken them in battle (due to the extenuating circumstances of the plagues motivating the Egyptians to fear the Israelites and their God and the favour upon them). What they had done was a lambano of some sort. Favour and the Egyptian's fear of the God of the Israelites motivated the Egyptians and their visitors who had heard of the mighty power of God to give them all these goods.

You are favoured to plunder

A person who has become a believer is a person born into the right family. Favour follows that person and people will be motivated to do a lot for the believer all because of the favour upon him.

Now they are those who do not even believe believers ought to have money even for the purpose of the word of God to be financed, these are babes in Christ. They do not really know who a Christian is yet Apostle Paul made it clear in:

2 Corinthians 5v.17
...if any man be in Christ he is a new creature...

The word 'new' is kainos in Greek. It means a new type of being *superior to the devil*. It means an unheard of creature.

Christians are not the poor trying to get rich. A Christian is a creature born with the right to wealth! He is born with favour following Him or her.

We are creatures of favour. We win because of favour. The grace of God upon our lives is the favour of God and wherever we are grace abounds and wealth comes to us because of this favour. Our Lord Jesus Christ walked with such power of Grace that He would be handed property without even asking for it. There are therefore a lot of principles we use to accumulate property or wealth and there is also a favour attached to principles that we can even get without dancing for it.

The plundering of the Donkey owner

The Lord Jesus Christ telling His disciples to go locate the donkey and colt does not prove Him to be a thief, any more than Jesus' disciples inquiring about and occupying an "upper room" makes them intruders or trespassers. It does not make them thieves either. It simply proves favour of the Lord upon their lives.

The whole event of the plunder of the colts is parallel to how I am not obligated to go home from church every Sunday and rehearse to my mother **everything** I did **in the emergency section or healing school**. In the same way, the Bible is not obligated to fill in every detail of every incident, including the one under discussion containing the colts. When sending His two disciples to get the requested animals, Jesus told them exactly where to go and what to say, as if He already knew the circumstances under which the donkey and colt were available. He did not say just go anywhere find me a donkey and bring it. No He didn't. Jesus may very well have prearranged for the use of the donkeys and even if he had not, the very meaning of 'Lord' is master owner so the other owner must have overshadowed by the Lord's favour that his spirit quickly got a hold of the Lord's need and wanted to supply without argument.

Furthermore, the innocence of Jesus and His disciples is reinforced by the fact that the disciples were able to leave with the donkeys. Had the disciples really been stealing the animals, the owners would not have allowed such to happen.

Notice after the use of the colts nothing is said in the Bible about what happened to them. For all we know, Jesus' disciples could have without more ado taken the colts back to their owners after their use. See, many people will try to find fault with everything they read, touch or get involved with.

Jesus did not steal. He is the master owner and favour followed him and still does those that are His followers in spirit and in truth that a colt will be something easy to ask and be given.

I remember way back when my car developed a problem. I did not even ask for a car, I was given one by someone who had seen the favour of the Lord upon my life. Favour follows a believer so that the plunder can have somewhere to stick to.

Alpha AND Omega

Let you mind think big and you will see big results.

Matthew 18 vs. 18
...Whatever you bind on earth it is bound In heaven...

Many people think the above scripture means that we do the binding first and God binds after us. That is not correct for God does not react; He acts - so this means God will have already bound these things we ask for WAY BEFORE we agree here on earth. Your mind should be settled on this fact!

God is the alpha and the omega. He is the great I AM meaning an eternal presence; the past, present, and future are alike to God. He sees the most remote events of past history, and the far distant future with as clear a vision as we do those things that are transpiring daily. He makes your end good before he tells you to walk it. God has already planned for you to succeed so thinking big is easy because the game ios already pre-planned just walk it.

We need balance

Someone said to me "Well now, I heard you say - you need balance in this". Yes we need balance because so many of our people only follow a preacher who treats God as an errand boy. Go and get a car and God goes. Go and get my house and God runs that is playing games with God. I have seen, heard and met preachers like that and God told me to quit listening. The moment they preach, I switch to cartoons.

The message for prosperity should rest in this fact: it should be wealth with a mission and to get it we need a paradigm shift. We need a change of thoughts.

Thinking like a wealthy believer

The wealthy, the Billionaire and the millionaire think differently to the average person, be it on issues of money, jobs, risks, sight, time or even investing.

Thinking On Jobs

The average person takes a job as a way to get wealth and if they do not get a job they think the world has come to an end. At the same time the wealthy know that a job will never make them wealthy. A job is not a tool to take over the wealth of the wicked and absolutely not a security like the average person thinks.

J.O.B. to me stands for the words **Just.Over.Broke**. A job is not the thing that can make you rich. Investment will. A job is to make a giving with but not to make a living with as many believers have done. Some can not afford to attend church because they will be at work most Sundays that shows their belief in God is limited. They do not completely trust God can take care of them.

Thinking On Money

The average person looks for ways to spend their money and also ways to save it yet the wealth mindset dreams of ways their money can serve them.

They are constantly looking for investments and not ways to save money like the average person.

Thinking On Risks

The average man lacks the mind that more risk is many times a sign for more return on their money so they do not take 'risks' at all. I placed risks in quotes because I believe there is a supernatural power plant in every spiritually active believer to avoid investments that will bankrupt them. However the word says if you do not take risks you are a lazy and an unproductive person;

Proverbs 22 vs.13
The slothful man saith, There is a lion without, I shall be slain in the streets.

Now the rich on the other hand understand beyond reasonable doubt that if they do not take risks then they will have already failed and can no longer make a big killing with their money. It all comes back to the way the rich think!

The bible says:

Luke 14:28
For which of you, intending to build a tower, does not sit down first and count the cost?

The bible here acknowledges that there are risks that we need to weigh and when we weigh them we get into what we want to do. The word is not saying that we should count the cost and fail to invest. No it does not say that. However for the believer there is a supernatural power plant in every spiritually active believer to avoid investments that will bankrupt them.

Thinking On foresight

The poor worry about today and do not have great vision for things in the future. They do hand to mouth jobs or businesses with no or little focus on the future.

The rich prepare today with an understanding of it bringing a good tomorrow. They think big about today. They value today.

Thinking On Time keeping

The poor waste time and think they have more of it. They never put enough thought on issues that have to do with time.

The rich know time is their biggest asset. You can take all the rich man's property or goods but I tell you if you give him time he will get those things back hundredfold.

Thinking On Investing

If you can think it up, you can bring it down. If you think poor, you will believe poor, act upon being poor and ultimately become poor. But if you think big you will believe big and obtain big results. If you cannot think it, you can't get it!

The poor think investing is risky so they do not invest much. The rich sees a ready key for gaining plenty so he or she invests more. In many areas there is a very defined level of how the poor think and how the rich think. They think very differently and as a result get very different results.

It is also in that thinking that a need to read more of God's word on wealth comes and it is through that reading and hearing God's word concerning wealth that faith to take over the wealth of the wicked is produced for wealth is according to your faith.

Chapter Four

Wealth according to your Faith

There is nothing called a money problem! All there is is a faith problem - the lack of it! It is not how much something costs BUT how strong your faith is to obtain it. The stronger your faith, the cheaper the things you want, even if it is in the figure of billions.

If you see a property worth billions, your first step should not be to look at how you are going to make that money because you probably would not be able to meet the billions needed to purchase the property in a short space of time or even in the long-term. So what your first step should be is to strengthen your faith. Wealth is according to how strong the faith you have is. It is not according to your bank account or your powerful credit scoring or rating. It is wealth according to your FAITH!

The stronger your faith, the more you can buy.

Romans 12 vs.6
> **Be it prophecy let it be done according to**
> **The measure of faith...**

Do everything according to the proportion of your faith. Never believe to live by faith without a job when you couldn't live by faith when you had a job. Whatever you are fixing to have, check on the level of your faith for there is nothing called a money problem to a child of God. The stronger your faith, the stronger your wealth base and your buying power.

Notice, God does not want you to have financial pressure. God is into you having financial pleasure. He wants you to possess financial power to do His work on the earth and so HE can increase and gain more ground. See. The word says it this way;

Psalm 35 vs. 27
> **Let them shout for joy and be glad that favour**
> **My righteous cause... let the Lord be magnified**
> **Which hath pleasure in the prosperity of His Servant**

God has pleasure in your prosperity. He did not die for you so you can be broke, busted and disgusted. Your faith will change your position. It will drive that poverty spirit until all you think about is how to favour God's righteous cause by financing it. When you start financing God's righteous cause God will come in. You SIMPLY CANNOT OUTGIVE GOD. When you surrender your best, God gives His best according to what has been given passionately. It is a matter of faith. It is wealth according to your faith. The wealth of the wicked comes to you according to your faith.

Make your faith work. Act upon what you believe. Talk like you have money. Talk and walk like an ambassador of the richest government and country there is. You are an ambassador of the Kingdom of heaven not from this earth. The scripture says;

2 Corinthians 5 vs. 20
We are ambassadors of Christ

This is the last time people will see you this broke! Give a shout unto the Lord!

The wealth of the wicked *is yours*. You are an ambassador of heaven and you should know that the devil stole your money. He controls the economy in the land you are a passer-by in and you have the authority to kick him out. Your faith will take the wealth. We are here to plunder the devil together and take back what belongs to us. Like I said earlier, he owns your bank, your workplace and the marketplace but that time is over for the new creatures in Christ have arrived!

Ambassadors of the Kingdom

Now, there is a British ambassador at the British Embassy in America. There is an American Ambassador at the American Embassies in African countries like South Africa, Zimbabwe, Nigeria, Ghana, Malawi etc. these ambassadors are paid by their home countries. It does not matter what the economy is like in their countries of duty. When the Zimbabwean, South African, Zambian or any other country's currency lose value, the Americans simply impose the power of their currency over the declining ones. They would see these countries struggle yet they will not be in any trouble at all as they are from a different country. Apostle Paul said this of us;

2 Corinthians 5 vs. 20
We are ambassadors...

Apostle Paul's point is that we being creatures from the beloved country of Heaven simply impose the power of our currency on all our problems and they will vanish. The power of our currency is faith. Faith is the currency of Heaven. We use it to soar above the world system no matter how bad the economy is in the place where we are. Because of faith, we can never cry that things are bad or the dollar is going down or I am white or black! All these are nonsense. The anointing produces through faith is a heavenly materiality that shows and favours no colour or background. The anointing favours faith. It responds to faith, so money or wealth is according to your faith!

Hope is not the currency. It is a goal setter not a goal getter like faith, so faith is a goal getter where hope is a goal setter. It is a currency that buys the goals that hope has set. Faith does not make sense. It only makes faith.

The distance between you and wealth

The distance between you and wealth is your faith. Many times you act upon what you believe and God sends a person. The thing between your faith and your miracle many times is a person. If you are believing God for money, God will send you a person to show you how to get money or simply hand you money like what many times has happened to my wife and I.

The widow of Zarephath wanted profit but God gave her a Prophet. Israel wanted to be free and God sent them Moses. God will provide for His people. We are His beloved. A new creation and a peculiar generation.

Notice; we are a new type of being that has just burst onto the scene. It is not for us to lack. Plenty is ours. *Riches belong to us, health is ours, we rule, we are not broke and the wealth of all the sinners we see is already stored up for us by our father in heaven. We are taking the wealth of the wicked* - Glory be to God.

The day Jacob plundered Laban

Jacob believed big and acted upon what he believed. He has faith. He knew how to lambano. He was a master thinker. He developed a mindset of wealth and used the power of faith to bring good thoughts of wealth and by faith he plundered Laban.

He first received it into his spirit (dechomai) then he acted it out (lambano); received as if by force. Jacob did something that the natural mind can never understand. There is no science that can really explain what happened. To the natural mind it did not make any sense but to God it made faith. Faith does not make sense. It only makes faith.

If Jacob was to deal with the devil in the natural, the devil would have prevented him from accumulating the riches of Laban. However Jacob kept the devil on this side of faith and by keeping the devil in the realm of faith, he plundered Laban. Look at how the word says Jacob took over Laban's wealth;

Genesis 30 vs. 37
> **And Jacob took him rods of green poplar**
> **And of hazel and chestnut tree; and pilled**
> **Before the flocks in the gutters in the**
> **Watering throughs etc...**

AFTER Jacob realised Laban's flock of animals (Laban's wealth), he saw that there were some speckled and some had spots on them and some were ringstraked. So he thought faith when Laban asked;

Genesis 30 vs. 31
> **...what shall I give thee?**

Jacob answered and said;
> **Thou shall not give me anything...?**

That was the answer of faith. Faith says God did something already. To Jacob, the war of his wages was settled in heaven above and Laban could not do anything about blessing Jacob; only God could and had already done so. What was left for Jacob to do was to do what God said to do in the realm of the spirit. Jacob gave this request in:

Genesis 30 vs.32 and 33
> **I will pass through all thy flock today removing**
> **From thence all the speckled and spotted cattle,**

**And all the brown cattle among the sheep, and
The spotted and speckled among the goats:
And of such shall be my HIRE...everyone that is
Not speckled and spotted among the goats, and
Brown among the sheep, that shall be counted
STOLEN with me.**

Speaking in the realm of the senses, Laban had an advantage over Jacob. But Jacob was out to plunder Laban with a supernatural wealth transfer that Laban had never seen. Laban was in for a surprise just like the devil will be when you wake up and take over his wealth. There is a supernatural speed that is welling up in you as you read this revelation and it is that power, that dunamis power in you that will give the devil hiccups when you start loading the wealth of the wicked.

Abundance is yours, quality is yours. Money comes to you. Supply is yours. Success is yours. The wealth of the wicked is yours just as it was for the Israelites when they plundered the Egyptians. Just as it was when Jacob plundered Laban. Are you learning anything? If you are, just look around you or go into the city centre or some place and look at all the banks, the buildings, all the properties and anything else you like and confess:

"All that is mine. The wealth of the wicked is mine in JESUS' NAME!"

You and the Plunder of Laban
Laban thought it was going to take long for Jacob to have enough but he was in for a surprise. The word of God says;

Genesis 30 vs. 42
> **The feebler were Laban's and the STRONGER Jacob's**

See! The feebler were Laban's and the stronger became Jacob's. God showed up with supernatural power that transformed what seemed to be a mess into a message and a test into a testimony. But if you come to think of how he did it you will understand that taking the wealth of the wicked is an act of God and God alone. Notice how God led **Jacob in verse 37**;

> **And Jacob took him rods of green poplar, and of
> Hazel and chestnut tree; and pilled White strakes
> In them, and made the white appear which was in**

The rods. And he set the rods which he had pilled
Before the flocks in the gutters in the watering
Troughs when the flocks came to drink; that they
Should conceive when they came to drink

There are two miracles here that one can not explain away. The first miracle is that the animals would take the colour of the white from the pilled white strakes of the green poplar, hazel and chestnut trees. The other major miracle is that which happened in verse 39:

...the flocks conceived before the rods and brought
Forth ringstraked, speckled and spotted

That supernatural speed of wealth take-over was upon the animals that the moment their mouths hit the water, the power of God welled up in the wombs of the flocks that some conceived right there in front of the rods and brought forth Jacob's wages. Do you see that?

That power is on you. It is on you to take the wealth of the wicked. I am not ashamed of this take over. The wealth of the wicked belongs to us who believe. We ought to drive the best cars, control companies, rule, lead governments so we can bring peace and comfort to people. The wealth of the wicked is not for a few but for every child of God. We are too blessed to be broke!

Jacob took over in verse 40!

And Jacob did separate the lambs, and set the flocks
Toward the ringstraked, and all the brown in the
flock Of Laban, and he put his own flocks by
themselves and Put them not unto Laban's cattle

Jacob plundered Laban because of faith. He believed that if he played around with sticks he would get a favourable outcome. But he did not end there, he acted upon what he thought and God honoured his faith. God is a respecter of faith and not a respecter of people. God answers faith. Jacob did not end on believing, he had to put sticks in the water and confess that when the animals came to drink they would take on the colour of the pilled rods and take up their colour and conceive right there in front of the rods. He supernaturally forced the animals to confess giving birth to the desired colour of animals. Yes sir, they did and wealth came to Jacob!

This was an instant miracle. The moment the animals saw the rods, they conceived in favour of Jacob. Everything went Jacob's side.

Now if I do this in this day and age many will brand me a magician or a man belonging to a certain cult. When we are talking wealth of the wicked taken over we are really speaking power, supernatural speed. We are speaking what seems impossible. Jacob took the best animals;

Verse 41 of the same chapter says
Whensoever the cattle did conceive,...Jacob Laid the Rods before the eyes of the cattle in the gutters, that They might conceive among the rods. But when the Cattle were feeble; he did not put the rods in the troughs.
SO THE FEEBLER were Laban's and the STRONGER were Jacobs.

Here we are talking supernatural speed and supernatural strategy. The conceiving was done at a supernatural speed right before the rods and at conception, but the supernatural strategy came way before the conception. It came by Jacob putting pilled rods into the feeding toughs. This is a miraculous way of obtaining wealth. It looks and feels like magic yet it is the word nonetheless. It works better than magic.

Supernatural speed in our life

My wife and I had visitors one day at our house and we had no money in the bank. Not even a dollar. Being people who confess wealth, holiness, health and everything bestowed upon us by the Almighty God, we started confessing money into our lives. We even asked the visitors what they wanted for supper but we knew there was nothing in the bank. Now folks who are out to put holes in what happened to us will be happy to hear this. They would say magic, pure and utter magic!
We had previously checked our balances and we found there was no money at the bank. We knew we did not have money coming in but did not know what to do except do FAITH; acting upon what we believed, I prayed a small prayer and made a confession:

"*I am a child of God so money comes to me so I can feed my church visitors. Now Lord Jesus Christ I thank you because I have money.*

So I am going to the cash machine to get some money. Devil you have lost as usual. In Jesus' Name, amen - I am not broke"

I started laughing poverty off me and laughed plenty in to my life and yes into the bank account.

My wife made preparations to cook – she even boiled some water, there was nothing much to cook, but we were acting upon what we believed and that is real faith. When we got to the cash machine, my wife put the bank card in the slot and according to our faith there were several thousands in that particular bank account. Now some might say that that does not make any sense at all, but whoever said it should make sense. *It only needs to make* FAITH!

We treated our visitors to a hearty meal and we had a good time in the Lord. As I made that confession, the Holy Spirit was moving someone to send us that money. The Holy Spirit was working to compel someone to give us what we needed and more.

Another day that I vividly remember is the day when we opened the doors to our then new ministry, I had no money to pay rent for the church building we had hired and I had already checked with my bank and realised I had no money to suffice. The following day was the day the rent needed to be paid and without it there was no way we were going to get away without being evicted from that building. After realising my predicament, I got on with my day and acted as if all was well. I even planned for the Sunday teaching as if I had money to be in that building. In the evening of that same day, I logged on to my internet bank account for what seemed to be the umpteenth time that week and checked the balance again and God had put exactly the figure that was needed. Now, this is not money that the bank could not explain - it had a source. They could explain where the money had come from but I realised that wherever it came from it was only put in the bank hours or just after I started confessing and acting as if I already had it.

Sometimes other financial institutions would give reasons like they just thought of doing a promotion and I was the recipient of a cash sum. This is not magic! Look at all the events in the word.

God is always involved in things you can not explain. Can you imagine the Egyptians simply handing in their jewels to the Israelites? Maybe you might think that this is possible without the power of God which brought favour to His people. But what about the visitors in the Egyptian houses also handing over their gold, silver and even clothes without a single question.

Imagine where the gold coin Peter got from the fish came from. If you can, that is where some of the money will come from. Where is this money coming from? I dare answer this with all gusto *"exactly where Peter got his when Jesus sent him to fish and take out a coin from the fish's mouth"*

This is the power of supernatural wealth transfer. With it you cannot be broke. You *will start preaching beyond borders and beyond your normal financial base. It is* marvellous!

This kind of favour should not be unusual to any child of God. I know a lot of times I prayed to have money and as soon as I open my eyes money will be there infront of me. From where you may ask; I dare answer this with all gusto *"exactly where Peter got his when Jesus sent him to fish and take out a coin from the fish's mouth"*

Wealth will come through principles that are well loaded with favour. Sometimes money will show up when you are in a tight spot. Money you will not be able to explain where it is coming from. It is the same as Peter getting a gold coin from a fish. *No one makes noise about that but when a preacher dares to preach that what happened to Peter can happen to you when you favour God's righteous cause - all eyes will be on him.* We should learn to put the limits off of God but always with a biblical balance.

God Unlimited is power realised

Psalm 78:40-41 says,

> **How oft did they provoke him in the wilderness, and grieve him in the desert! Yea, they turned back and tempted God, and LIMITED the Holy One of Israel.**

That is a powerful. Verse 41 says they limited the Holy One, which is speaking of God. That's an amazing statement! The dictionary defines the verb "limit," as "to confine or restrict within limits." We can confine, restrict, or limit God in our lack of faith. That's a totally foreign concept to many people. Many people think there can be no such thing as a limit on God. They see that as removing His divinity. A God that can be limited isn't really a God in many people's thinking. However God gave us will power so we can limit Him by our faith for He only responds to faith.

I will say this: God isn't personally limited by anything or anyone. But when it comes to us receiving from Him, we can limit what He wants to do through us or for us. God doesn't 'sovereignly' do what He wants with us. We have to co-operate. God Himself is limitless, but what He can accomplish is limited - Not because of any lack of power or ability on His part, but because of the part we have to play.

Ephesians 3:20 says,
> **Now unto Him who is able to do exceeding abundantly**
> **above all that we ask or think, according to the power**
> **that worketh in us...**

Many people stop after the first comma and proclaim God can do anything, but that's not the truth of this verse. God has limited Himself to what we believe Him to do. If there isn't the power of faith working in us, then He will not, work without us. God is who He is, regardless of what we think or believe. If we don't believe God is real, that doesn't make Him cease to exist. As far as our experiences go, we won't encounter Him until we change that opinion.

Take salvation for example. Second Peter 3:9 says, "**The Lord is... not willing that any should perish, but that all should come to repentance.**" You can't make it any plainer than that. It is not God's will for people to perish, but they do. Why? Not because God wills it, but because God gave them a free will and they choose to reject God's provision for their salvation.

Most people don't want to be responsible for their lives. They like to think that God just 'sovereignly' makes things happen in their lives. That way, they can blame God for the mess they are in and say, *"God is teaching me something or making me a better person."* But that's not what God's Word says. If God is teaching you something in your poverty then its either God is a foolish teacher (of which He is not) OR you are a very big liar (of which you are). If it was God teaching you then you would have learnt it along time ago but if it is you then being broke all this time shows you are a very foolish and very slow learner.

Now listen; God is not teaching you anything in your poverty. All there is to it is you are poor and you don't have any other person to blame so you finally have decided to pin the blame on God and if I be plain with you - that is the spirit of the devil making you do that. The Lord willed for the Israelites to enter into the Promised Land in a short period of time. But the generation that came out of Egypt died during the forty years in the wilderness. That wasn't God's will. That was their own choice. They fell into disobedience and God was not obligated to save them.

There are many ways we limit the Lord. In Psalm 78, the scripture mentions:

...they limited God... by not remembering His goodness and faithfulness toward them. They lusted for things they didn't have, and rebelled at Godly authority.

You have power to cooperate with God

Think of Jesus sending Peter to take a coin from a fish's mouth. Where did the fish get the coin? Some might say "Oh Jesus is the son of God, He can do anything", but they forget that the word says:

Philippians 2 vs.7
> **He emptied himself and took up the form of a Servant (or human)**

Jesus emptied himself of His abilities as God and became our example by becoming one of us. In fact he said:
John 14 vs.12
> **Greater signs shall ye do...**

Do you see that? If you still have a problem with this just remember that the Lord Jesus Himself said:

Matthew 18 vs.20
Where two or three are gathered in my name
There will I be in the midst of them.

What has that to do with my argument that it can happen to you? I would answer everything because Jesus is there when I agree with my wife about money issues because His word said He would. And if He is present then I know it's about Him not about me.

If He got a coin from the mouth of a fish then that means - He can put money in my pocket. Many people fear to talk about this, they are afraid of being labelled holy rollers or magicians. Never be afraid of the word. If the word says it, I believe it; I act upon it and THAT SETTLES IT! Lambano (seize by force) the word of God and never fear.

Think of Jacob's plundering of Laban. How can animals conceive when they see pilled rods? What power was that? You can never get wealth if every time you try to explain the chemical composition of a miracle. It is unexplainable. If it is explainable then it will seize to be one see! Even if I had no explanation of how it happened, I wouldn't care less. I am a son of God and I should have His best for my life so I can preach His gospel to every creature. I am ready for wealth with a mission. I do not forget why I need to have the wealth. I concentrate on the purpose of wealth and not the wealth itself and my faith works because of my focus.

Psalm 62 vs. 10
...When wealth increases set not your heart on it...

My mind is alert. I am not envious of sinners. I simply have a revelation that whatever they have is mine, but I can't get it by robbing them for God has a divine strategy to take over the wealth of the wicked people of this world. God has a strategy for this great wealth transfer.

If I see a sinner with a bank, I will start up my own even right next to his and his customers will become mine. The anointing will attract the clients of the bank that belongs to the wicked into my own bank. I know a certain preacher who owns a bank and I am buying his shares in order to promote this wealth transfer. I want to bankrupt the devil. Glory be to God!

Feed on the word for wealth to flow

Be addicted to the word. That is the only addiction God finances. If God's word says it, believe it, act upon it and that will settle it.

God can not go back on His word. His own word is a law unto Himself; He cannot go back on it. He can not break it. God is bound by His own word to perform it. He is, as it were, a prisoner to what comes out of His mouth. Notice what David says about God and His word;

Psalm 138 vs. 2
...You have exalted your name above all names and You have exalted your WORD above all your name.

David says God made it that His name which is above every name be it poverty, cancer etc is lower that His own word. God made His word to control even what He Himself wants done so that if He says to you

Proverbs 13 vs 22
...The wealth of the wicked is stored up for the just...

That is exactly what He has done for He exalted His word above His own name. Apostle Paul also shows us that God even seeks counsel from His own word. This is not to be taken to mean that God runs short of ideas to the extent that He looks for ideas from His own word. No, it does not mean that. All it means is that God does exactly what is in the confines of His word.

Some folks said "Oh Pastor you can't say that because God being God can do what He wants even if it is not in the confines of the bible". The error of these people was to think that God worked in some mysterious way that a believer can not really comprehend. That is a mistake! It is true God can do anything that He wants to do BUT the 'anything He wants' is already written in His own word that there is no need for Him to do something outside the word He exalted above His own name. The bible has many books; surely a brilliant father would write what he wants done in that many books!

God respects His word and it is from hearing and reading this word that faith to take over the wealth of the wicked comes. No wonder He says;

Ezekiel 12 vs. 25 God says in short that;
He watches over His word to perform it...

And on to proclaim that;

Psalm 89 vs. 34
The word that has gone out of my mouth will I Neither alter nor change...

This is not a promise. This is a divine fact. God wants you to know that you can trust His word just as He trusts it. If God can be trusted then His own word can be trusted. You have to take it as it is. Swallow it hook, line, sinker, the fisherman and his boots!

From His word comes faith and faith is acting upon His word. Many people get it wrong by thinking faith comes by hearing the word of God. That is not true. There is no bible for it. **It is true** that without the word of God there is no faith BUT the bible if read clearly will show you that *faith comes by hearing. It is the hearing that comes by the word of God* but before you choke on me let me show you.

How faith for wealth comes

Romans 10 vs.17
...Faith comes by hearing, and hearing by the word of God

Take a look again at the above scripture. Now, that scripture does NOT say "faith comes by the word of God"! No, it does not say that at all! *It says Faith comes by HEARING. It is this HEARING that comes from the word of God* that would develop faith. Before explaining the central part of increasing faith which is the HEARING part lets take a look at:

Romans 10 vs.17
FAITH comes by HEARING, and HEARING by the WORD OF GOD.

Three things are mentioned here, which are FAITH, HEARING and THE WORD OF GOD. So without one of the three there, one is not near faith. If you remove hearing you will be left with word of God that is not HEARD and no faith WILL COME. Some might say how can the word of God be ineffective? Yes it can, the Lord Jesus himself had this to say;

Mark 7 vs.13
> **You have made the word of God of non effect by your**
> **traditions...**

Having the word of God in front of you does not automatically give you faith see. So it is possible to make the word of God of no effect if we do not act upon it. On its own the word is powerful but our response to it can make the word of no effect in our lives. If you remove just one of the above three from the others, you are left with one powerless entity.

Notice here; when you get a hold of the real meaning of that scripture then it will be very easy for you to have a revelatory knowledge of what to HEAR the word of God means. That is why the Lord Jesus Christ said:

Luke 8 vs.18
> **Take heed how you hear...**

He also said In Luke 6:46 **"But why do you call me 'Lord, Lord' and do not do the things I say"** You have to act upon what you hear otherwise it will become belief only. Believing and faith work together but they are not the same. See!

Hearing the word of God and acting upon it is how you increase faith be it for finances or for healing. Acting upon what you hear is the HEARING that brings faith. For faith to be strengthened one needs to be a doer of the word not only a listener like what James 1:22 says:

Remember to **"take heed how you hear"** because what some consider hearing is in actual fact simply listening. Hearing is acting upon the word in order to produce faith. We agree with God when we hear him correctly.

Agreeing with God

Apostle Paul says;

2 Corinthians 3 vs.18
...but we all with a open face beholding the glory of God as in a mirror are changed from glory to glory Are changed.

The words 'are changed' mean to be *metamorphosed*. As the word of God comes to us and we see it as a mirror; we look at it and know who we are then we are changed into another man. We are changed to a higher level. The word has to say it. We have to locate ourselves in the word. The word says we;

Galatians 2 vs. 16
...are made JUSTIFIED by the faith of Christ...

Then the word also says;
The wealth of the wicked is stored up for the JUST

So that means that we the Just according to the word of God have access by faith in the Lord Jesus to the wealth of the wicked. No arguments here!

We simply agree with God in our spirits, actions and access is granted to the stored up riches. Miracles of wealth and the wealth transfer will be ours when we become one with God's cause and stay addicted to the word. That is the only addiction God sponsors.

We behold God's promises in His word to us and agree with it by locating ourselves in the word then the wealth of the wicked is attracted to us. We become wealth recipients and magnates of resources. We start to locate ourselves in the wealth of the wicked!

Locating yourself in the wealth of the wicked:
The woman and the prophet

A certain woman, widow of a prophet came to Elisha and spoke to him about a need in her life. She was in a very great need and in a very bad situation. Her husband had died and left a loan to be paid off. She had no means to pay the money back and she was also struggling for her own livelihood. Creditors came to her and wanted to take her two sons as slaves for the money her husband had owed. Now before I go further let me say God is not into making us borrowers but lenders. He wants us to be lenders. You may ask why?

Because His word says we are no one's slave. If we are ever going to be servants it should be to our Lord and for the Lord. See:

Proverbs 22 vs.7
> **The rich ruleth over the poor and borrower is slave to the lender...**

This woman was now a slave to the lenders. Instead of her being the lender she became a borrower. In fact her husband was and it affected the family.

The widow had just suffered the loss of her husband and had no one to support her, she had no wealth to sustain herself and her two sons, had a debt that needed to be paid off. On the other hand the lenders were threatening to take her two sons. She had nowhere to go to and no one to help and she came running to Elisha, the man of God and told him the situation she was in. She had located herself in the word. She recognised who Elisha was and how she was going to get help...asking the man of God.So Elisha said to her:

2 Kings 4 vs.2;
> **What shall I do for you? Tell me, what do you have in the house?**

And she said:
> **Your maidservant has nothing in the house but a jar of oil.**

Human efforts can only go so far and he did not have what it took to humanly help the poor woman but with God we make strides in the Spirit and those strides come into our lives and affect the natural. The woman had to agree with the man of God. She also had to locate herself in the word of God that came from the man of God.

When Elisha asked her, **Verse 2** says:
> **What shall I do for you? Tell me, what do you
> have in the house?**

Elisha was looking for something I call a 'hold'. Something that God can use in the life of that widow to redeem her with, some seed that can be used to produce a deliverance for that poor widow. By seed I am talking of something that you can thrust into your future so that when you reach that future you will find it in a greater measure.

Now, the woman answered and said,**Verse 2** says:
> **Your maidservant has nothing in the house
> but a jar of oil.**

It was so insignificant and so miniscule compared to the great big need she had. That presented a situation of potential loss of her two sons until the next Jubilee. She faced a situation that could not be humanly solved. The woman located herself in the word of God and removed all impossibilities. She had nothing at all with her, except a jar of oil. Not money, not jewellery, not any treasure, not goats or sheep, not any camels or costly items that she could trade with – all she had was a jar of oil!

Then the Word of the Lord came to Elisha and he said

> **2 Kings 4:3.**
> **Go; borrow vessels from everywhere, from all
> your neighbours—empty vessels; do not gather
> just a few. And when you have come in, you shall
> shut the door behind you and your sons; then pour
> it
> into all those vessels, and set aside the full ones.**

The widow knew how little oil she had and how that little jar she had was more than enough to contain all the oil she had. But praise the Lord that she also knew the power in the Word of God as it goes forth. She recognised her power was limited without God so she located herself in God's word and believed God with no questions asked and that location she had of herself in the word gave her a miracle.

When we locate ourselves in the word we become enjoined with the word. People will not be able to tell you apart from the word and the devil will not be able to separate you from the word.
Do not ask how. In fact get the 'HOW?' out of here!

The widow did not ask how all this was to come to pass she simply kept and went away and just did what Elisha had asked her to do. So she went from him and shut the door behind her and her sons, who brought the vessels to her; and she poured it out. (II Kings 4:4) What a miracle, the oil kept flowing as if coming from a bottomless jar and it filled all the vessels she and her sons could borrow from their neighbours. Vessel after vessel kept overflowing being poured into from a little jar. The woman also plundered her neighbours. She asked for many jars and they gave her with no question. She was now operating in the realm of favour.

The little jar of oil was perhaps insignificant in the eye of the widow but what she had had brought what she did not have. She was not giving into any doubt whatsoever for she had believed the report of the man of God and located herself in to that word. She was simply determined, determined to obey the Word of the Lord with all her strength and all her might.

If you can simply locate yourself in the word the seed for your miracle is right with you. Submit to the Lord and surrender the little that you have, you will see that little seed produce a mighty fruit for you even today. The wealth of the wicked which will be used for greater work of Christ will be given into your hands.
When God asked Moses, he was willing to drop the little rod he had in his hand on Mount Horeb and that eventually became the rod of the Lord that enabled him to do mighty exploits. The widow at Zarephath was willing to make a small cake for the prophet Elijah before making any for herself or for her son and received the miracle the man of God had proclaimed with the flour and oil never failing until the end of famine. Whatever the Lord is asking you to do today, simply obey and you will see the mighty deliverance. Just get the 'HOW?' out of your life and start budgeting for the wealth transfer.

Budgeting for wealth or writing a vision for wealth?

The bible does not concentrate on writing a budget. It simply says **"write the vision down"**. You are a new type of creature that writes a vision down. You are raising a vision and not a budget. See! For you success is normal and lack is abnormal.

There are a lot of children in the things of the Spirit who are constrained by their budgets. A vision is what Christians write and not a budget. A vision is like a budget but the difference is it has God above your expenses. A vision first calculates what God commands like the tithe and the offerings. It removes it and gives a figure of what the Lord will be given in that month or that year and it removes that before all the other things. A vision then sees what your future will look like and creates a seed from your income that can catapult you into that future and only after that can it move you into what you need in the flesh. Yet some calculate what God will need from their carnal budget and they think they will make it in to heaven. Never will they make it for God should always be first and if we trust God then our carnal budgets should turn into visions. Budgets if given priority over a vision will leave you with a headache and no tithe to pay to God and no offering. Why? Because you will never have enough money to give God if the world becomes your first choice. A budget takes the world as first choice. A vision takes God as first choice and God says whatever *you put above him is your God so if your car insurance is paid before your tithe then the insurance company is your god. If your house decorations are done* without considering God's commands and what His work needs then the decorations are your God.

It is simple sometimes to see who will make heaven and those who will not. How? You may ask...just find people who put God first in their lives and you have heaven bound Christians and find those who treat God as an after thought then you have hell bound Christians. It is very simple!

People need to put God first even in their finances and believe that He will supply where they lack. If believers do not do that then why are they called believers? Believers ought to believe what God says. See!

Now the widow gave her vision and not a budget. Creditors came to her and wanted to take her two sons as slaves for the money her husband had owed. When Elisha asked her what she had, she said she had one jar of oil. Elisha then told her to borrow as many jars as possible from her neighbours and lock herself in her house and start pouring oil from the one jar into all the other jars. The widow did exactly as Elisha has suggested. The oil filled all the jars. When she'd run out of jars, she asked her son for another but he told her there weren't any left. The oil stopped pouring. Elisha then told her to sell the oil, pay off her debt, and live off the profit.

Favour vs. laziness

Now when we talk of favour, we are not talking about being lazy. Look, the woman got the oil miraculously as I have obtained money and goods miraculously in my life but still the prophet said; Sell the oil, pay off the debt, and live off the profit. The prophet literally said 'go and do a little business'.

Again when Jesus was talking to his disciples about buying goods, He told them to; **...Sell... their coats**
You ought to be in business. Don't sit around and think these things will come while you are asleep - God does not play voodoo games. He is not into magic.

The woman and the miracle

Now, I read the story in two ways: as literal and symbolic. Closing the door symbolises not taking notice of appearances or listening to common sense or any criticism. Common sense would tell you that one jar of oil cannot fill 30 or 40 jars or even two. The widow had faith in what she couldn't see. She is also described as a "woman of the wives of the sons of the prophets unto Elisha." This means she had already witnessed the power of God being expressed through Elisha, so she had faith in the God of Elisha. If you can celebrate the gift upon your man of God you will have what he does!

Now if the widow had a million jars, the one jar of oil would have filled all of them with more to spare. So enlarge your capacity to receive. Get the 'HOW?' OUT OF HERE and with everything in you create faith boosters for wealth!

Chapter Five
Faith Boosters for Wealth

Faith boosters for wealth are everyday ways of boosting or extending your faith to take over the wealth of the wicked.

Faith is not something the child of God has to get. The child of God already has faith. The problem is not whether or not you have faith but HOW STRONG YOUR FAITH IS.

Romans 12 vs. 3
God has dealt to every person the measure of Faith

We all started out with the same quantity that is why the scripture above says 'the measure' and not 'a measure'. This means that we are all given a specific amount of faith when we come to the Lord but it is up to us to increase on it.

This does not mean that we need more faith - that may shock you, but all you need is to strengthen the one that you've got. **Faith is like a muscle**, the more you practice it the stronger it gets. It is like the thing in your head called the brain, you don't need to go to a meat market to look for more brains to put in your head. You can't say to the butcher *"hey Mr Butcher, could I have two pounds of brain so I can add up on my brain power"*. No, that would be down right mad. What you need is to study so you can strengthen your mind with the right information.

This is the same with faith. There is nothing called few faith, there is weak faith. There is strong faith and there is great faith, and as you have already seen, wealth is according to your faith. Wealth is not attracted by education. Wealth is attracted to faith and the cure for weak faith is faith BOOSTERS; everyday ways to stretch your faith.

The weaker your faith, the less wealth you will attract so there is need to develop or identify everyday ways to boost or amplify your faith. Abraham, who is the father of faith, used faith boosters for wealth and these were provided by God.

Faith boosters in Abraham's faith

When the Lord appeared to Abraham and told him that he was going to give him a son he also provided faith boosters so Abraham could be reminded of God's promise to him. These faith boosters were always in front of him and above him to the extent that there was no way he could forget what God had said. Look at this:

Genesis 22 vs. 17

I will multiply thy seed as the stars of the heaven, And as the sand which is upon the sea shore; and thy seed shall possess the gate of his enemies...

Every night when Abraham saw the stars in the heavens - the promise of God was magnified in his mind. It boosted his faith. Everyday Abraham would see sand or every time he went to the beach - the promise of God came running into his spirit and extended his faith. That amplified his faith. It tickled his ability to act upon what he believed.

When God said He was to multiply Abraham's *"seed as the stars of heaven"*, God was referring to us Christians. We are from above. When He said He was also going to make Abraham's seed,

As the sand which is upon the sea shore...

He was referring to the Jews and these two types of people are here on earth today as a result of Abraham's faith being amplified by the faith boosters God brought in to His delivery of the message to Abraham. You might say how can sand represent the Israelites and the stars represent Christians- here is your answer in

1 Corinthians 15 vs. 47 - 49;

The first man (Adam who is the great grandfather of the Jews) is of the earth, earthly: the second man is the Lord (the second Adam who is our father) is from Heaven. As is the earthy, such are they also that are earthy and as is heavenly (meaning believers) such are they that are heavenly

The sands of the earth symbolised the natural descendants of Abraham which are the Jews, but the stars of heaven represented the spiritual man which we are. The stars referred to us believers and this entire big plan came to pass as a result of Abraham believing God. Acting upon what God promised was enlarged in Abraham as a result of faith boosters.

The name as a faith Booster

God did not just tell Abraham about what was coming. He changed Abraham's name which was Abram before. Abraham means "father of all nations". This man had no sons or daughters yet every time a person would mention the name Abraham it reminded Abraham of the promise God made him. There was not a single child, they were old and the bible concurs Sarah's womb was dead. This did not make Abraham waver.

Romans 4 vs. 20
...he did not stagger at the promises of God, neither did he consider the deadness of Sarah's womb...

Do you see that? Abraham did not stagger. He had too many faith boosters to stagger. Every time he would look up, he would see the stars and they would remind him of the promise of descendants God had made to him. The moment he would step foot out of his house and set his feet on the sand, it boosted his faith. It amplified his trust that the promise God made would come to pass and it did. That is the power of faith boosters.

The word as a faith booster

You might need faith boosters if you are like me. In fact any Christian who has no faith booster is a weak Christian. To say it like it is, any Christian who does not use biblical faith extenders is not a Christian. Why would I dare say that? This is because Christians ought to have faith boosters that would let their faith soar high enough to possess the wealth of the wicked and anything they need. Another reason is that any believer who says they don't need faith boosters - do not really know what faith boosters are all about.

The word of God is the greatest faith booster so if a believer says they are too mature that they do not need faith boosters - they are simply lying through their teeth. All Christians need the word.

If you don't have the word you cease to live the Christian life for we feed on the word. Apostle John said all the miracles were written so that

...all may believe...

See that? All the miracles Apostle John recorded he says are for our benefit. They are simply faith boosters. The word is a faith booster. This tells you;

Titus 1 vs. 2
The Lord cannot lie...

Now, if I believe Titus then that scripture will be a faith booster if I keep saying it to myself. When I read Psalm 68 vs. 19;

Blessed be the Lord who LOADETH us with Benefits...

I know that Psalm is true because I know God wouldn't be lying since Titus says He cannot lie. So in this case this is the faith booster. It is a reality that all believers need. We need to feed on the word daily and trust that God cannot lie. So whatsoever He says will come to pass and whenever we say scriptures out with our mouths, we boost our faith. We extend our faith. We will start acting upon what we believe and our faith is strengthened for faith 'cometh by hearing and hearing by the word of God'.

Daily faith boosters

I know I used to write what I expect to do for God or what God promised me on small pieces of paper and that used to act as my faith boosters. I used to do this so that every time I see those little papers I soak into the atmosphere of what I will do for God and what God promised me daily. That doesn't mean I had dementia. It doesn't mean I used to forget too quickly. It simply means faith boosters create a consistent atmosphere to soak into the promises of God daily!

I remember writing down that I was going to be a citizen of a certain country that had strict immigration rules. I wrote that down (if you don't write it down somewhere it remains a wish) but if you write down this they become decisions. The word of God concurs in Habakkuk 2 vs. 2:

Write the vision down so that who sees it may run...

Every time I saw the paper I had written this on, I knew that my family and I were going to obtain citizenship in that country. We had difficulties at first. The immigration office kept turning us down but I did not stagger - I had too many faith boosters. Here I am not talking about things like handkerchiefs. No I am not. Things like handkerchiefs are points of contact and I believe when one is mature in the things of the Lord God Almighty, they would not need other points of contact but they would still need faith boosters - at least one; the word of God. That booster is a must! When you are grown (mature) in the things of God the word, becomes the major faith booster.

Regarding the subject on Points of contact, the same is not so with faith boosters, we need faith boosters. The word of God is the greatest faith booster. Here we stood upon the word of God and every time I saw that paper I wrote the promises of God on, I reminded myself of the fact that we would get the citizenship. These papers were not magic wands. They had no power of God in them whatsoever. All they did is write a mental picture. The faith boosters kept reminding me of God's promises and in due course we got the citizenship! Praise the Lord! The word says;

Psalm 103 vs. 2
Do not forget His benefits...

In my bible I wrote; *"my bible says it, I believe it and act upon what I believe and that settles it"*. Every time I open my bible I see it and it has struck a cord in me so much that now that I am mature in the things of God, I do not use other faith boosters as much as I did anymore. The word of God as it is is now buried deep in my heart that it is mainly the booster I use.

The other booster that I can not leave is my children. I received angelic visitations where I was told the names of all my children. All my children were named by the Lord. In these two visitations I was told by the angel what they were to do when they reach the age suitable for them to be in ministry. So when I am with them, I am reminded of God's goodness. When I call their names I am reminded I was told their genders AND names way before they were born and one of them I was shown the whole delivery process and what would happen seconds after birth. I saw it that now when I am with them or with one of them, something in me automatically reminds me that Satan is in trouble. My children are a faith booster for me.

Faith boosters do not bring faith

The term faith booster does not necessarily mean faith bringer. Only the word of God is a faith bringer. Faith boosters will remind you of what God said and in turn what God said will strengthen your faith. See!

Wealth can come by faith boosters. Find scriptures on taking over the wealth of the wicked. Find scriptures that cover the faithfulness of God and speak them out to your self. Confess them to yourself until every fibre in you, every cell of your blood soaks into the fact that;

The wealth of the wicked is stored up for the just...

See what will happen to you if you do this. You will speed up the take over of the wealth of the wicked in your life. When you find scriptures that cover your case with regards to your finances, you will see finances come to you from various directions. It will shock the world. You will be a wonder, not just one who wonders. Faith boosters for wealth are necessary. When you are walking in town, look at the bank, businesses, cars etc and confess even under your breath.

"The wealth of the wicked is mine"

When you do that those buildings, cars etc will become automatic faith boosters that whenever you see them your mind will not register it in the usual way. You will just find yourself murmuring;

"I own that in Jesus name. I own it to spread the gospel with it. That is my story. The wealth is for the believers in Jesus' name!"

These faith extenders are day to day ways of amplifying your faith. If you come to think of it, the Israelites were told by God to make burnt offerings everyday. Think of the smell of the burnt offerings going up to God daily. They would smell it when they woke up, they would smell it when they ate, when they went to the restroom and when they were going to sleep. In fact the smell was the order of the day. It became part of them that the idea of God bringing them out of Egypt was real to them. They soaked into that reality. The smell was the faith booster. It was a daily faith booster.

Numbers 28 vs.3-6

> **And thou shalt say unto them, this is the offering made**
> **by fire which ye shall offer unto the Lord; two lambs of**
> **the first year without spot day by day; for continual burnt offering. The one lamb shall thou offer in the morning and the other lamb shalt thou offer at even;**
> **...it is a continualburnt offering**

A continual burnt offering served two purposes. First, as an offering to God and second, as a FAITH BOOSTER. Wealth is no different; we need a faith booster for wealth. In this new covenant as was in the old, the word is the best FAITH BOOSTER.

Chapter Six
Supernatural Debt Cancellation

If you spend more than you bring in; you are in DEBT. If you continue to spend more than you bring in; you are worsening DEBT and if you never deal with your debt; you are in DEBT CRISIS. DEBT is also the abbreviation for **Doing Everything But Tithing!**

Debt is a Trap

Why is debt a trap? It's a trap because debt enslaves you. When you go into debt, you lose your freedom.

Proverbs 22:7 says:
> **The rich rule over the poor and the borrower is servant to the lender...**

Any time you take a loan or some credit, you in a sense become a servant to those people. You become mentally enslaved to them. You may wake up at night worrying about how you are going to keep up with your bill payments. You become physically enslaved to them. You end up working longer and longer hours to meet your obligations. And you become legally enslaved to them, ultimately responsible in the eyes of the law to make your payments. It becomes a trap that many people never get out of. Debt crisis is like food poisoning. It will kill you whilst you are enjoying. However, no debt problem is unsolvable for there is a supernatural debt cancellation.

When folks hear things like supernatural debt cancellation, their 'lazy antennas' stand on end. They think magic. Far from it; Supernatural debt cancellation is a way to cancel your debt God's way and with His backing. There is a host of principles to cancel debt that is protected by God's favour. Supernatural debt cancellation involves the word through and through.

Just before the wealth of the wicked

For the wealth of the wicked to be gathered to you - you must know how to pay off your debt and how to stop accumulating more debt God's way. If you don't, you will spend a lot of time trying to make a living that there will be no time to make the gospel reach the ends of the world through you. You need to pay your bills. There is a supernatural debt cancellation. Notice what the word says;

Philippians 2 vs. 9, 10
He inherited a name that was above every name...
That at the name of Jesus every knee should bow...

Your bill has a name and your bill's name is under the name of Jesus. In the name of Jesus your bill will bow. Just don't tell God about your bills, tell your bills about your God. Tell your bills how BIG God is. They will listen. If you have bills just do a little dance for Jesus right now and shout 'It's over!' because the time of living in debt is over. You are entering the land of 'debt free!'

For you to fully enter and abide in this land of the debt free, you ought to follow a few steps.

Be in control: Temperance

See what the Lord says here though His word;

Proverbs 23 vs.2
If you are a man given to appetite PUT A KNIFE TO YOUR THROAT

For you to get out of debt there is a need for you to control your spending. This does not necessarily mean you no longer get the same things you used to have. All it means is you might need to spend less on the same things. You need to take control. According to the word of God you need to *put a knife to your throat* if you are given to appetite. That does not mean kill yourself. It simply means temperance or 'Enkrateia' in the Greek meaning – to control or hold yourself by the hand of your spirit!

A revelation of debt cancellation

The Lord spoke to me about this supernatural debt cancellation and showed me in His word the principles for debt cancellation. When I was shown that a certain scripture I considered alien to the subject of wealth could be used to include wealth, I argued with Him about it until He proved to me that the principles work for wealth as well as healing and in general godly living.

Now before He gave me the revelation and the scriptural basis for it, the Lord did a wonderful thing that caught my attention - He went ahead of the scripture and showed me the result of what will happen when the principles are followed. Here it is as the Lord showed it to me:

2 Peter 1 vs. 8
> **For if these things be in you, and abound,**
> **they make you that ye shall neither be barren**
> **nor unfruitful...**

See. When the principles I will show you in a few moments are lodged inside every fibre of your being they will make it that you will never *fall or be broke*. But if these principles are not in you the word has it that you will be blind spiritually and financially too. Look at the scripture:

2 Peter 1 vs. 9
> **But he that lacketh these things is blind,**
> **and cannot see afar off**

Again if these principles are in you and abound, they help you neither to be broke nor lack opportunities to take over the wealth of the wicked and increase resources for the kingdom. Remember it is money with a mission. Now opportunities will knock on your door when you adopt these principles. This is exactly what Apostle Peter was given by the Lord:

> **For so an entrance shall be ministered unto you**
> **Abundantly...**

Principles for debt cancellation

In **2 Peter 1 vs.2-11** the word says;
> **Grace and peace be multiplied unto you through the**
> **knowledge of God, and of Jesus our Lord, According**
> **as his divine power hath given unto us all things**
> **that pertain unto life and godliness, through the**
> **knowledge of him that hath called us to glory and**
> **virtue: Whereby are given unto us exceeding great**
> **and precious promises: that by these ye might be**
> **partakers of the divine nature, having escaped the**

> corruption that is in the world through lust. And beside this, giving all diligence, add to your faith virtue; and to virtue knowledge;And to knowledge temperance; and to Temperance patience; and to patience godliness; And to godliness brotherly kindness; and to Brotherly kindness charity.For if these things be in you, and abound, they Make you that ye shall neither be barren nor unfruitful in the knowledge of our Lord Jesus Christ. But he that lacketh these things is blind, and cannot see afar off, and hath forgotten that he was purged from his old sins. Wherefore the rather, brethren, give diligence to make your calling and election sure: for if ye do these things, ye shall never fall: For so an entrance shall be ministered unto you abundantly into the everlasting kingdom of our Lord and Saviour Jesus Christ.

The steps given by the Lord to Apostle Peter are very valuable if one is to get out of debt God's way. These are not principles I got excited with a few months ago and decided to teach. No, they are not. This revelation is the one I live by. It is this revelation that made me get out of debt and I also gave many to use in getting out of debt.

The Lord told me to teach these so as to prepare those who will take it for the greatest wealth transfer. This transfer is knocking on the doors of those whose ears are ready to hear. Prosperity is knocking right now and the body of Christ needs to respond. They need to wake up and smell the money!

Explaining the principles of supernatural debt cancellation

2 Peter 1 vs.6 says add
        ...to knowledge TEMPERANCE...

Enkrateia

The word temperance is **ENKRATEIA** in Greek. This means 'to hold yourself from within.

Man is spirit, possesses a soul and lives in a body but many times the body rules the man. The spirit should be the boss, the soul should be the supervisor and the body should be the worker.

However, for temperance or ENKRATEIA - holding yourself from within to happen, there is need to let the spirit be the boss like God made it. The only way to do it is to suppress the body like Apostle Paul said in 1 Corinthians 9 vs. 27

I keep under my body...

Your body has many requests that are contrary to the spirit, contrary to taking over the wealth of the wicked and would want those requests met no matter the day or time. If you manage to be temperate (enkrateia) you will win the battle and be able to control your spending. It is the body that spends and not the spirit. See!

ENKRATEIA yourself: hold yourself from within. Put God first and never spend more than you bring in if you are not led of the Lord. That would be getting yourself into serious debt. Don't continue to spend more than you bring in, that would be worsening debt and if you never deal with your debt you are in debt crisis.

Take control of your spending. Cut back on luxuries until such a time when the wealth of the wicked is now in your grasp. Appetites should be reduced. If you like extra special designer clothes wait until a time when shops have a sale or something and buy your yearly clothes. Just after Christmas in January and February, many shops in most countries have very good price reductions. This is the time to buy clothes for all seasons. Don't buy things that you cannot pay for. The Lord said "if your eye causes you to sin pluck it out", and His word also says:

Proverbs 23 vs.2
If you are a person given to appetite put a knife to your throat...

When the scripture says put a knife to your throat, it does not mean to literally commit suicide. No it doesn't. It simply means you need to limit your appetite for things. Take control of your spending. Limit your spending. Spend only when it is necessary. There will come a time when you go into a shop without a thought of whether or not your card has enough credit on it.

Hold yourself from within. Hold your body by the hand of the spirit. ENKRATEIA yourself!

Knowledge

Luke 16 vs.11
**How can you have the things of heaven if you cannot
manage unrighteous mammon (money)?**

Your management of money can also be a good indicator of how good you will be with the things of the Spirit. Don't start casting out demons from bills. For one, demons do not live in bills although they influence them, and all bills need is to be paid. If you pay them - the lenders do not trouble you.

Find knowledge on how to pay your bills and how to reduce your debt. Get into lessons that teach you how to manage your debt until you become a debt free person. In all your lessons remember you are a believer and a believer writes a vision and not a budget – put God first no matter your debt because it is God who will get you out of debt and transfer you from there into the land of wealth. The little that is coming in should be kept in a clever way not in a way that feeds the wolves in sheep's clothing.

Beware of thieves who pretend to represent God.

There are thieves, wolves in sheep's clothing who are on the scene - some with breathtaking miracles and to be plain they also have money-taking miracles. Some do not even mention money in church but they do not rebuke people because they are afraid of losing them. Like I keep saying, they steal other people's sheep and never discern why those people have congregated around them.

There are so many extreme teachings on prosperity, from the grossly ignorant teachers who liken Mercedes and Rolls Royce's to godliness to those who teach that Jesus was poor. The whole point is that money was not an issue to Jesus. He didn't live in abject poverty nor in the presidential suite. He had enough to do what God needed Him to do on earth, and that's the goal that we should be trying to reach.

Papa Hagin, my spiritual father, spoke against the grossly erroneous, cancerous teachings of some charismatic leaders and some preachers in other areas and other so called non denominational churches on "firstfruits" and other topics. See, some have gone to extremes...selling the anointing oil and all. Some even sell clothes or say the anointing process is not enough until one sends an offering. That is daylight robbery.

I am not at all against offerings and blessing the Man of God but there are extremes that need to be avoided. As a matter of fact, there is no other way to get a harvest without a seed but should the seed be money always? No it should not always be money....your time can be a seed. The word of God is also a seed that produces faith. Money is also a seed and is one of the best seeds.

Now when papa Hagin started attacking sin along this line, I know of one church in particular which refused to put his book the MIDAS TOUCH, which dealt with extremes, in their bookstore even though they have publicly proclaimed Hagin's teachings prior to this book.

However when men,

1 Samuel 2 vs. 17;
    . . . abhorred the offering of the Lord.

In the days of Samuel, the glory left. And the glory left during the healing revival when people became "disappointed and hurt by the excesses of some of its leaders. Money became the focus and not the Lord.

Too many began to love money and glitter more than they loved God and the true riches that come only from a humble and deep walk with Him. Many casualties were chewed up and spit out by a system that shook them down for every penny in their pocket, promised them blessings that never quite came, and then blamed the victims as the cause of their own downfall.

In this day and age many are taught good confession yet with no right morals. They are taught a faith that simply tries to get but not the one that also makes a person become a vessel of love.

I remember people that I well respected who got chewed up by this system. They just decided to call us and utter obscenities and shouting at the top of their lungs that they did not want anything to do with us. At first they were a holy ghost filled, sanctified people and within a few months they became chewed up by a system that shook them down for every penny in their pocket, promised them blessings that never quite came, and then blamed the victims as the cause of their own downfall. Told them the right confession but left out the morals.

This is not a get rich quick scheme, we are already rich.

What knowledge should give people is the fact that there are miraculous ways of getting things from God - biblical prosperity is not a get rich quick scheme. Miracles of finances like getting money from a fish's mouth are meant for tight situations that God immediately - pronto- wants to do something about it. Prosperity by taking the wealth of the wicked is a lifestyle of commitment, giving and obedience to God and carries a reason - to spread the word of God with the wealth.

Prosperity is not about money.

Prosperity is less about money than it is about freedom to do what God puts on your heart to do. That is part of "the word of faith" that Paul preached (Romans 10:8).

That is exactly what Brother Kenneth Hagin who made an impact in my life, Smith Wigglesworth and many of the giants of our faith taught. This teaching has now been "hijacked" by radical abusers of the sheep that even those that were right are put under the same blanket. But the devil is a liar!

Get knowledge on money. Use that knowledge, for revelation is not the truth you know but *the truth you use*. Do not let people steal your money by sending you mediums like handkerchiefs, water or little pebbles. These will not work if you miss a step or two in the process to your 'breakthrough', all which include sending money to the man of God who sent you the mediums.

Diligence

God is not interested in you working hard or overtime. He would rather you WORK SMARTER. Diligence is not hard work. It takes diligence two minutes to do what hard work would take four hours to achieve.

In financing the kingdom, there is a need to understand that debt cancellation should not be confused for debt consolidation. Consolidating or putting your debt into one bill by letting a lender pay off your debt is simply hard work. You create yet another bill by paying someone else to take care of your already long list of people you owe money.

Diligence would simply make sure it has made all the necessary ways to pay the bill. Diligence will be temperate. Diligence will have knowledge on what is owed and creates a plan on how to pay back and not delay payments. Diligence has wisdom enough to understand that if you spend more than you bring in; you are in DEBT. If you continue to spend more than you bring in; you are worsening DEBT and if you never deal with your debt; you are in DEBT CRISIS.

Don't rob Peter in order to pay Paul - It is a mistake no matter the status of your credit rating or scoring. Some folks think having credit worthiness is something to enjoy so they accept anything offered to them but with diligence you will realise that if a company calls you credit worthy, it is actually another way of saying you **ARE WORTH PUTTING INTO debt!**

The commercials on TV and radio all suggest that we should get what we want right now, and many of those ads even offer to finance our desires! Instant gratification programming permeates our desires for material things and becomes a dangerous trap for our finances. The result is millions of people drowning in debt struggling to rob Peter in order to pay Paul yet God says be diligent, renew your mind and be in faith - act upon the word and you will take over the wealth of the wicked.

Add virtue to Faith

Now let's begin with what is meant by "virtue". Virtue is the Greek word **arête** pronounced "**ar-et'-ay**". In the New Testament the word translated virtue, when describing Jesus' virtue in Mathew 5:30 and Luke 6:19 and 8:46 is a different word meaning *dunamis* or mighty power of God. Virtue (as given in the book of Peter is defined as relating to valour, excellence, praise, or virtue. It is an outward evidence of something inside a person, which can be clearly seen as a quality of character.

Virtue therefore as given by Apostle Peter is the commitment to have morals that show the Lord Jesus in us. It is the desire for godliness, out of a love and gratitude to God.

Now for debt cancellation, morals should be of great importance. There should never be shortcuts to wealth that involve stealing or dealing falsely for that is not virtue. If you are a believer, examine yourself see if you are not given to bad behaviour that will cause the word of God to fall in to disrepute. Adding to your faith virtue is part of your obedience to the gospel of God's word. Obedience to God attracts wealth and money goes to whosoever understands it.

To temperance add patience;

It is wonderful how Apostle Peter was led by the Holy Spirit to start by temperance which is **ENKRAETIA** - holding yourself from within - to patience. This shows that holding yourself from within is short lived without **patience**. Patience gives comfort to hope being the goal setter until faith which is the goal getter comes.

In debt cancellation patience is required. Do not chew more than you can swallow. There are many arrangements you can make with those you owe and in these, arrange for long periods of payment as long as there are no big interest rates.

A man in my ministry followed this revelation and his bill for five thousand was given a repayment period of ninety years without interest. However by faith principles he managed to pay it all in two of the ninety years.

Now this world is full of get rich quick schemes designed to make you feel you can obtain riches and wealth overnight with little effort on your part. These schemes are contrary to God's plan. God's plan for prosperity is patience that is why He says:

Wealth hastily gotten is easily lost...

Enkrateia yourself and stay in patience. Your wealthy place is already here.

And to patience godliness

Godliness here indicates that you not only do the right things because God says you must, but you do them because you truly love God and wish to honestly please Him in how you act and think. When you are living in Godliness, you are doing the right things because you know them to be right. You long to be like Christ in your daily living and in how you think about others and treat others.

Godliness in my life reaping results

One day I took my Mercedes Benz to this garage for repair and told the man to give me a rundown of the parts that were needed before he did anything to the car. As you would have guessed the man went ahead and touched my car before he gave me a rundown of what was needed and phoned me with news that he had broken a certain part of the car. This he did because he thought that if the parts were expensive I was going to give the job to someone else so he told me he broke the part that made the car not even start. So I could not even take the car from him even if I wanted since he had broken the part that was essential in making the engine function. I simply responded by reminding him that I had told him to touch the car only after he told me the parts that were needed but he had not done that, now he had broken a part of the car that was very essential.

Adding patience to godliness I did not give the man a hard time when he told me that I owed him for the part he - himself had broken and some imaginary five hours that he said he worked on the car.

I simply went to his garage, paid for that part and the labour and took my car and left with a smile on my face. I did not even say one bad word BUT that night the Lord Jesus visited him and he phoned me early in the morning and asked if he could meet me at his garage. He told me in that office how he has not suffered like he did in thirty years of his profession as a garage owner. He related to me that all night he could not sleep and wanted to give me back my money including the new part he had replaced and told me what had happened with the car. I begged him to keep the money but he flatly told me that part of me leaving the money with him was not negotiable because of what happened to him all night long. An angel had visited him many and told him he had to give me back my money for he had lied to me. He had done a mistake and was not willing to go another day with that

107

money. He gave me back the money plus more all because godliness called the God of the breakthrough into his house.

In short, he had touched the wrong car!
If believers would simply add patience to godliness, they would have all their wrongly made bills cancelled and their other bills eased or even erased. A lady sowed just a measly fifty pounds into our lives and got bills worth about ten thousand pounds cancelled within nine days of her sowing the fifty pounds. Add patience to godliness.

...to godliness brotherly kindness...

Brotherly kindness suggests being a servant toward others for love's sake, to be kind, generous, charitable and courteous to others. I find it interesting that brotherly kindness follows godliness. This means to me that having the right motive, which is Godly love, certainly gives birth to a flood of good deeds to fellow mankind - brotherly kindness.

Brotherly kindness can get bills paid very quickly. As you love those around you with a godly love, those people will bless you back. It is a very simple principle that is why God says:

Give and it shall be given unto you...

good measure...shall *man* give

Man will give you if you give them. This giving might not be in money but when you give God can cause other people to open doors for you.

...and to brotherly kindness charity...

Notice that Peter says you should not only have a little bit of a Christian character showing, it should abound. In other words, behaving like Christ will become more and more natural to you. It is regrettable that the King James uses the word 'charity' for 'love' for that word does not really represent what God is really communicating to us.

Now you can't stress the importance of real godly love. You can not overdo it. This kind of love does not stem from your feelings or emotions. The word says:

1 Corinthians 14 vs. 1 Amplified
> **Eagerly pursue love... make it your aim, your Great quest...**

Godly love allows you to love even the worst of your enemies, even people who meant you harm. Godly love will give you the strength to forgive them and mean it. It will cause you to be a distribution centre and in return;

Luke 6 vs. 38
> **Give and it shall be given unto you a good measure shaken together and running over shall men give out of their bosom.**

Like brotherly kindness - If you are a person of Love, people will be compelled to give you and love to be around you. You become a contagious Christian. Your love expressed will show its fruits in return. No mistake about it.

Now, it turns out that in verse 8 Apostle Peter places a very powerful sentence. Even verse 9 is another strong statement. Peter says here that any Christian who lacks "these things" is having a vision problem. They lack vision or foresight. Not that their physical eyes are the problem, but rather their spiritual eyes need a check up. The eyes of their faith will be dead.

Either you are not seeing yourself for who you really are, or you are not seeing the scriptures correctly, or both.

Verses 10 and 11 are meant to encourage you. It's Peter's way of reminding you to get busy striving to be Christ-like, for "if you do these things, you will never stumble and an entrance will be supplied to you abundantly into the everlasting kingdom of our Lord and Saviour Jesus Christ."

These things if created they will help in understanding the seed faith that many have failed to understand and that many have also used to rob their people.

Chapter Seven

Laws of Wealth Seed Faith

Genesis 8 vs.22
> **As long the earth remains seedtime and harvest...
> will not cease**

This declaration was given to our father Abraham, his household and to all creation by God Himself. God said as long as believers sow seeds they will harvest - come what may. As long as the earth is still here, seed faith will be here.

Notice, the scriptures say seedtime and harvest and not harvest time because as far as God is concerned any day can be payday.

Isaac, when he dwelt in Gera at the time of famine, and when everyone was leaving town for Egypt where there was food - he sowed in that land and got a hundredfold. He sowed in a land of hunger and reaped more than was expected. In fact people of that land were packing for greener pastures. God wanted Jacob to forget the world system and come over to the God System. God said to Isaac:

Genesis 26 vs.3 TLB
> **Do as I say and stay here in this land. If you do, I
> will be with you and bless you...just as I promised
> Abraham your Father**

Genesis 26 vs.12 TLB
> **Then Isaac sowed in that land (with famine) and
> received in the same year an hundredfold**

God is the one who told him to stay in a land with famine. Why? Because according to God seedtime and harvest remain as long as there is the earth. Payday for the sower is any minute. Anytime can be harvest not harvest time. Any day can be payday and no matter how hard it is payday will surely come!

However this is where the biggest mess has come in.

What is wrong with the law of the seed?

Focus and motivation are the things that are wrong with the 'seed faith'. Some of the people who have hijacked this truth command people to "Sow a seed of $1000 (or any amount) into my ministry today, and God will give you back a 100-fold return in money" Now if this verse was true then preachers and Christians alike would be not just be billionaires or millionaires but real Quad-trillionaires in a few months. Sure we reap what we sow but that does not mean it should be restricted to monetary value only. How do I know this? Malachi 3 vs. 11 proves it;

I will rebuke the devourer for your sake... If you sow that is. Many preachers are fully aware of the kind of people they are exploiting. They know it makes them money to keep repeating this money for money giving. How sick it all is. As Jesus said in:

Matthew 23 vs.14
Woe to you, scribes and Pharisees, hypocrites! For you devour widows' houses?

What many have called the "Seed-Faith" teaching is a distortion of 'Sowing and Reaping', which is a biblical concept. But when it is distorted by preachers and sold as a means of "Giving to get" then it has gone well beyond the scriptures. The purity of simply "giving from the heart" is lost and replaced with selfish motives. People give because the preacher "guarantees" they will get a 'big return' on their investment!

The motivation is so wrong that it is no wonder that this doctrine has produced disastrous fruit in the church. It is one of the sickest things around that people only give to get. Look, I am not saying giving to get is wrong. All I am saying is the sower's main focus should be on supporting God's work and not on treating Him as a vending machine in the sky or an investment avenue where you sow and get with no love for the one you are giving. Focus and motivation for giving should come back to sowing and repeating if it should be seen to be working.

If we say giving to get is wrong even if the focus and motivation is not getting we will be very wrong for what farmer sows without expecting a harvest. To ask such a situation will be the same as to ask a farmer "*I know why you are sowing, you want to reap you don't you trick man?!*" Yes he wants to reap that's why he sowed BUT if the focus goes on harvest only with no clear purpose for sowing being established it is evil. The purpose should be to further the Gospel of Christ and should never be done grudgingly. The word of God says:

2 Corinthians 9 vs.7

Every man according as he purposeth in his heart, so let him give; not grudgingly, or of necessity: for God loveth a cheerful giver.

The tithe is not negotiable yet it should be given cheerfully. The offering on the other hand has no percentage but should be given and given cheerfully.

Look at your giving as an act of worship. Make sure you are motivated by love, by the desire to be a blessing, rather than the desire to get. Then name your seed. If you do, you'll be in line for a blessing. If you don't, then you're letting the devil control what belongs to you.

Those who steal shall be judged!

I shudder to think of the fate that awaits some of these preachers on Judgement Day and at the same time I shudder to think of what happened to those who do not give at all for they are robbing God Himself. The preacher will be robbing people and faces judgement on that basis. The people of God steal from God by not supporting God's work in their churches.

Some preachers ask people who are not members of their church to pay tithe to them. that is robbery. The tithe is paid to your local church and not the other way. There are also those that have partnered with other churches but have not partnered with their own church. Here the reward is on rebuking the devourer and not on hundred fold. Another thing is the bible also speaks of a thirty-fold return, a sixty-fold return and a hundred fold returns.

The motivation for giving is not so much to bless that ministry, but to GET SOMETHING BACK from God. The motivation is all twisted. Do they really expect God to "bless" something so wrong-hearted?

Sowing also becomes thievery when people tell you to give them a specific amount for an exchange of the anointing. They can tell you the amount that they claim the Holy Spirit has told them BUT the question is which 'holy spirit?'

Where do I sow?

Galatians 6 vs.7
> **Do not be deceived, God is not mocked; for whatever a man sows, that he will also reap.**

This scripture has been used wrongly for many years. It is usually used by preachers to warn unbelievers and by other Christians when they are angered by other people. However, this is not the main purpose of the scripture for one verse before that, we see this scripture that tells us exactly where to sow if we want to reap what we sow. See it for yourself:

Galatians 6 vs.6
> **Let him that is taught in the word communicate unto him that teacheth in all good things.**

The word "communicate" in verse 6 is used to refer to financial support see:

Philippians 4 vs.15
> **Now ye Philippians know also, that in the beginning of the gospel, when I departed from Macedonia, no church communicated with me as concerning giving and receiving, but ye only. For even in Thessalonica ye sent once and again unto my necessity. Not because I desire a gift: but I desire fruit that may abound to your account. But I have all, and abound: I am full, having received of Epaphroditusthe things which were sent from you, an odour of a sweet smell, a sacrifice acceptable, well pleasing to God. But my God shall supply all your need according to his riches in glory by Christ Jesus.**

To communicate on giving to Apostle Paul's need was what the letter to the Philippians was talking about. This is not about stealing from people of God but the people of God need to understand that they can not escape offerings and tithing just because they fear that the preacher would spend that money on. What the preacher does with offerings and tithes has nothing to do with the tithe payer. If the preacher misuses the tithe or indeed the offering that will be between them and God. All you have to do is never stop tithing and giving to God.

Now if you are not a tither and you do not give offerings there is no hiding it, you are a *thief* and you are in fact stealing from God Himself and that is not a joke. The truth needs to be told.

What you sow is not even your money; it is God's money after all. See, it is God who gives you seed and you in turn trust God by giving Him part of the seed He gave you first so that he can take care of the rest.

God gives you the seed to sow

2 Corinthians 9 vs.10
...he ministers seed to the sower...

What happens first is God ministering seed to the sower. You sow, and then God gives you the seed to keep sowing. Its fair enough, God gave us everything including our first seed but for a return to take place, what is needed is to obey the law of the seed. The law of the seed says if you sow a seed, God will give you in return. From that wealth, He gives you plenty more to make a seed out of. So you give and God gives His measure. You give and God gives plenty more seed for you to sow.

Tithing as a seed
Now, when one says they are in D.E.B.T, abbreviation for Doing Everything But Tithing and Doing Everything But Thanksgiving, they are really confessing their point of weakness. This might seem funny to some but God is not laughing for He says;

Malachi 3 vs.8
You have robbed me in tithes and offerings

Many people have always known that a tithe is a must but few realise that the scripture actually says;

...Tithes and Offerings...

...ARE A MUST! Tithes and offerings are a must because God wants His house to be full of resources. In fact He also says;

Malachi 3 vs.10
...so they may be food in my house...

His main purpose for implementing tithing and offerings is so as to bless you and chiefly to get resources into His house so the gospel can fully be financed. If God can not get it from you, He will not get it to you. If He will not get it through you, He will not get it to you.

What if it's not God's will?

Someone came to me and said, "Pastor, I don't believe that everyone is meant to be a billionaire" well I told that person that I believed that too to her surprise.

"but you said if we give tithes and offerings God has promised that He will give us blessings we won't be able to receive" she said.

"Rich doesn't mean billions only- it can mean trillions or you can choose to have plenty for you and to do God's will". To be wealthy does not mean to be a millionaire. It simply means having enough to share with others. It simply means you are supplied!

A man came to me and said; "what if it's not God's will to get you rich?" Many people who say this have not yet realised that the will of God is not guess work for the real child of God. It is not something He whispers in the ear of a chosen few. No sir, it isn't. No ma'am it is not. The will of God is the Word of God. It is the bible that has God's will. As you have already seen it - His will says:

Proverbs 13 vs.22
The wealth of the wicked is STORED UP for the just

So it is no longer -"Do I know the will of God", BUT simply "I opened His will for me and read: The wealth of the wicked is STORED UP for me"

"Sir", I said "it is God's will; He has just told you that when you tithe He will. In fact God has already provided the riches all you need to do is to get busy getting wealthy.

Malachi 3:10
...Pour you a blessing that you will not have any room to Receive.

If you can't contain a million then God will give it to you. If a billion sounds like its something you cannot contain - when you tithe and give offerings with a cheerful heart and a good focus and motivation then that billion is yours. He will give you what you can't contain. So whenever you think something is out of your reach and you know you are a tither and offer passionately and are living a holy life - then you are the right person to get that 'unobtainable' amount of wealth. It is simple but hard to take in.

The man continued to say, "Sir, if it His will then why am I not a billionaire already?" The man had not heard about thinking big, acting upon what you believe the difference between faith and believing, the creation of a wealth mindset, lambano and dechomai, supernatural debt cancellation or even wealth according to one's faith etc.

Now this man was looking at me with the eye that said "I got you preacher man!" he was one of those believers who believe that God is in control - we don't do anything at all. So realising this, I looked at his head and his hair was not combed so I said; "if God is in control he would have cleaned your suit and combed your hair". Glory be to God he saw it and realised he had to **lambano** the blessing of God. Before we were done speaking we had sorted his problem of not tithing and the combing of his hair.

The value of Tithing

Some people doubt the value of tithing. If anyone ought to doubt tithing and offering's blessing, why do they believe in salvation? It is the same gospel. That is just a mess the devil took to the pulpit to prevent the purpose of tithing that God implemented. All God is doing is;

...So they may be food in my house...

If you are not tithing and giving offerings, you are a thief. You are a robber and there is no excuse. Stop stealing from God. God wants you to prosper but the principle of tithing and offerings can not be removed. You need to know that reality whether you hate it or not. ***Tithing is of God that is why the devil will never tempt you to tithe or to give offerings.***

There are around 331 **ifs** in the bible that deal with 'if you do this, God will do that'. If you pay your tithe and offerings (notice and offerings) God will but the motivation should not be getting but the furtherance of the gospel. See;

Malachi 3:10
> **Open the windows of heaven and pour you a blessing you will not be able to receive**

When He says He will open the windows of heaven He means that He will open your eyes so you see a business idea. He will give you a pick in the things that will give you wealth and not pour out of heaven MONEY TO BUY MANSIONS. No, that is not what He is saying.

Naming your seed

Naming your seed is not naming your harvest. I tell God what my seed is all about and he decides what the harvest will be and how big it is going to be. The harvest can come as a business idea or a certain thing that can provide for the need you had when you sowed.

The widow in Elisha's life needed money but God provided a business idea. God's nature is a nature to give. The Bible says, *God so loved the world that He gave.*

Let me help you. Many times people sow, give and tithe, but they never name their seed. Because you never named your seed, you probably don't know what you have put in the ground. So how are you to know whether it is to come back to you 30, 60, or a hundredfold. However, the 30, 60 or hundred fold is according to what God chooses. It's not always for money to money, house to house or watch to watch.

According to that Scripture in Galatians, whatsoever, you put in the ground is going to come up. So we have to consider our ways and give thought to what we are sowing. If you consider what you're sowing, then you'll begin to recognize your harvest.

Blind Bartimaeus called out to Jesus

Mark 10 vs.47 to 52
son of David have mercy on me.

Jesus said;
...what do you want me to do for you?

What a question. Jesus according to Hebrews is the one who created the world and everything in it including Bartimaeus himself, yet He was asking what Bartimaeus needed. How could He ask such a question when He had eyes, let alone the supernatural knowledge to know that the man was blind and needed to see?

Jesus wanted Bartimaeus to speak out his need. See! There are more than eight thousand promises to the believer in the word, so God wants you to mention what type of blessing you need among the eight thousand promises. This is not because God does not know what you want but He simply wants you to confess and speak out your need with your own mouth for there is power in your own word. Name your seed!

It is not all wrong to wrap your seed with expectation

Wrap your giving with expectation but that should never be your focus for God's work should be your focus. When you wrap your giving with expectation be specific in what you want the Lord to bless you with but do not tie Him to those specifications. However God is a God of specifics. In the book of Acts chapter 3 we see Peter and John healing a crippled man;

Acts 3 vs.1-10
A certain man lame from his mother's womb was carried, who laid daily at the gate of the temple which is called beautiful; to ask alms of them that entered into the temple.

This man had EXPECTATION. He did not think healing. He would hear the preaching in the temple everyday whilst begging outside. When Peter and John came along - moved with compassion ignored his request for money and went straight to the issue of healing. Peter and John by saying **'silver and gold have I none'** does not mean that they could not put alms together and give the man.

Peter and John were simply saying your request is wrong. Your request is the reason why you couldn't be healed. Your motivation is wrong and your focus is very wrong. It is obvious that Jesus had passed this place often but the man did not want healing. He was thinking money. How do I know Jesus and these two disciples had passed by him many times before Peter and John prayed for him to be healed? That is because the word says;

...lame from his mothers womb was carried, whom they laid daily at the gate of the temple...

This man who was lame from birth was laid down at the gate to beg for money daily, not healing. His request was wrong. What motivated him was not a healing that would have made him well enough to fend for himself. He named his seed - alms and not healing. So all he was getting was silver in small quantities.

When you name your seed, name it right. The Spirit of the Lord should be involved in naming your seed. When you name your seed, name it with a focus on spreading the gospel with your harvest for God answers you with a harvest that is according to His will. The harvest you receive will be according to God's word.

Faith decides timing

Years do not decide what you receive. Peter followed Jesus and mumbled some words behind Him;

Matthew 19 vs.27-29
    Lord we have forsaken all to follow you

Jesus didn't say *"what, you mean two boats and all that fish?"* no, instead Jesus said;

Whoever has left mother or father for my sake will receive a hundredfold in this life...

All Jesus was saying was your seed determines what you will receive. He was implying that your seed put in today will catapult you into your future. Your seed will put you to be the head and not the tail.

By this I am not saying timing is not important but just that your seed determines the time of your miracle - continuous miracle, for it is harvest and not harvest time. It is very important to get your timing right.

Timing for wealth

Timing is of great importance because many times we miss it along this line: Timing for miracle is like timing for the right person to marry...we wait for 'Mr Right' or 'Ms. Outta Sight.' We wait and we wait and then wait some more, then we doubt if there is anyone out there for us. So we decide to have a little fun with 'Mr. Okay-For-Now,' and end up hurt, out of money and lonely. Next we spend some time with 'Ms or Mr. Too-Good-To-Be-True,' discover that she is or He is too good to be true, and leave with an empty wallet. 'Mr. Almost' and 'Ms. Pretty-Close' come along, but the more we get to know them, the further from us they become. This happens even in accumulating the wealth of the wicked.

All the time, brethren, blessings lie in our ability to realise the move of the Holy Spirit in our finances. Timing as a divine principle, calls for believers that can recognise the time and power of the move of God. We are called to ride a wave of the Holy Spirit and not to create one for ourselves. God is continuously creating wave after wave of blessing manifestation, all we need to do is recognise the wave and ride it if we ever want to take the wealth of the wicked. See, the moment you accept this truth; a wave will have started in your life. Just ride it.

Do you remember what happened to Elijah when he was in a cave at Mount Carmel:

1 Kings 19 vs.11-13
And he said, Go forth, and stand upon the mount before the LORD. And, behold, the LORD passed by, and a great and strong wind rent the mountains,

and brake in pieces the rocks before the LORD; but the LORD was not in the wind: and after the wind an earthquake; but the LORD was not in the earthquake: And after the earthquake a fire; but the LORD was not in the fire: and after the fire a still small voice. And it was so, when Elijah heard it, that he wrapped his face in his mantle, and went out, and stood in the entering in of the cave. And, behold, there came a voice unto him, and said, What doest thou here, Elijah?

The prophet heard the powerful wind and thought God was in that wind. Because of wrong timing on the part of this dear prophet, my bible says God was not in that wind. The rumblings of an earthquake came to Elijah's ears and he assumed that God was in the earthquake but again my bible says God was not in that earthquake. The third time He assumed God was in the flames of fire yet my bible confirms God was not in that fire.

It was only until a small; still wind passed by that the scriptures said 'God was in that small wind'. The word also says"

Genesis 8 vs.22
As long as the earth remain, Seedtime and Harvest remains.

When you have seed faith, the speed of accumulating the wealth of the wicked is increased but it is with great timing that you know when and where to sow that seed in the first instance.

People ask me if prayer helps and some spend day and night praying to get things from God. They arrange all night meetings so they can get things from God. They tithe, they sing, they pray but nothing changes. Is there something wrong with praying? No Sir!

Wisdom for money

Prayer alone does not bring money. If it did, then Bill Gates – one of the richest men on earth would be an intercessor. No he is not. There are principles that should be followed. Even where the prayer of faith is involved one needs to act upon what God said for money or wealth to come to them as aforementioned. They should pray but

still need to act upon what they believe. They need wisdom.
"Wisdom is the principle thing and in all your getting, get understanding" says the word in Proverbs 4:7. Wealth comes to those who yield to wisdom for as aforementioned wealth goes to where it is understood.

To some, seed faith is simply a way to get preachers rich but that is where they miss it. My wife and I are big time sowers. We help believers with money and we are also preachers of the gospel, teachers to be exact. We even house some at times and we are directors of a charity organisation helping people with needs so we know a thing or some things about the value and rewards of giving and as you might have guessed; we know giving is the right path to receiving.

Believers should not be greedy; there is no need to salivate over wealth. Our driving force should be solely to use our money for soul-winning purposes. If believers have faith in order to just have a fat offshore bank account and driveways that overflow with cars they will be missing it. The seed faith is there so that;

Malachi 3 vs.10
There may be food in GOD's storehouse...

It is not so that you can run and stand at the top of a mountain and shout;

"He fills my yard with cars, my garage runneth over" This maybe becomes good if you are blessed and are helping others to get to your level or even higher.

Wealth is for a way bigger purpose than that. When you give, God will give back. He made it that way and believers should never be ashamed of it. Just because we have:

Matthew 7 vs.15
...wolves in sheep's clothing...

That should never be an excuse for not giving towards the great commission for it requires money to be accomplished. Sure enough, the gospel of Christ is free to anyone but the way it is brought to the people is not free. Money is needed for buildings, PA Systems, Cameras, Utilities and many other things. The gospel is free but the means we bring it to the world is not. Wisdom to understand this will help you become focused on the right thing and when your focus changes from selfish to God's work you are set to take over the wealth of the wicked.

The seed should be sacrificial

The seed you sow should be sacrificial. If it is not, then you are tipping God and paying the world.

Psalm 126:6 says:
> **He that goeth forth and weapeth bearing precious seed,**
> **Shall doubtless come again with rejoicing...**

The seed should be sown no matter the conditions. It does not matter what your bank balance is - you have a seed!

Don't procrastinate.

Don't procrastinate and think that you can sow as little as you like as long as you are sowing. The amount is not the issue here. What matters is that you are sowing something sacrificially. If you are not then you ought to know that the seed you are sowing is exactly what the Holy Spirit is telling you not the one you convince yourself God has told you to sow. Never procrastinate for the word says;

Ecclesiastes 11 vs.4
> **If you wait for perfect weather, you will never sow.**

Plant the seed no matter the time, day, decade or weather because by you reading this book a wave is already in motion praise the Lord! Water your seed with a constant confession of God's word and acting upon what you confess and then see as plenty starts coming to you. Notice here;

Luke 6:38
> **Give and it shall be given unto you a good measure,**
> **Shaken together, pressed down and running over**
> **SHALL MEN GIVE...**

Do you see who will give you in return when you give? The word does not say "and God will give you". No, the word of God does not say that. It says "...men will..." give to you. This shows that when you plant a seed like tithing, offerings and all kinds of giving, the Holy Spirit will compel men to give you as a result of your giving. There are other accounts when miraculous things you can not explain will happen. This has happened to me many times. I would pray with my wife and money would just appear. Some times the lenders would miraculously cancel my bill even though I was paying in the right way and in an agreed way.

God does not want you to struggle; you have a seed!

God does not want you to struggle. He does not want you to spend a lot of time looking for a dead end job trying to make ends meet that there is no time left for you to fellowship with Him. That is not God's plan for His children. You are not created to struggle.

God wants us to live in the abundance of His resources and have much more to bless others with. When you give start to expect the best from a big God. You have a seed for your job will never make you rich. You job is not for a living but for a giving. When you treat a job as for a giving and not for a living your seed will protect you by God's power.

Protection by seed faith

Proverbs 3 vs.9-10
> **Honour the Lord with thy substance, and with the first fruits of all thine increase. So shall their barns be filled with plenty and thy presses shall burst out with new wine.**

There is protection that comes when the law of the seed is followed. However many of God's children do not give their first fruits. Some joke and say we don't get paid with fruits and we don't have barns either, so that refers to the Old Testament folk.

Have you ever wondered why people fight the revelation on giving by saying it belongs to the Old Testament? This is because believers are broke, disgusted and discontented. They have no money so they don't want to think about anything that 'takes' from them yet in God's system it is different. The world system says you *save money in order to get more*, BUT God says *you give and you will get*. Barns are your bank accounts.

When first fruits (the 10%) are brought to God, He protects the 90% He gives you, that way it can produce more. See this scripture;

Romans 11 vs.16

If the first fruit which is the 10% be holy, the lump is
 also holy, and if the root be holy, so are the branches

Genesis 8 vs. 22 has already said;

As long as the earth remains, seedtime and harvest... will not cease

The law of the seed is an all-time law that can not cease. It goes beyond testaments as you shall see. The word says

Ezekiel 44 vs. 30

And the first of all the firstfruits of all things, and every oblation of all, of every sort of your oblations, shall be the priest's: ye shall also give unto the priest the first of your dough, that he may cause the blessing to rest in thine house.

Are we not under the law if we tithe?

This is one question that has been used by those who do not want to tithe but the word can not be removed from because of what reprobates and stingy people want the word to say. However if one is not sound in the word they may think they are right. Why? Because if we are commanded to tithe today then it would seem to be away from God's command. Remember these reprobates choke the verse in:

Galatians 2:21

for if righteousness comes through the law Christ died needlessly

And since the word says the law was a tutor, in other words it would seem that the law taught us to give tithe in the Old Testament yet

here in the New Testament **Galatians 3 vs.25** says;
> **...now that faith has come we no longer need a tutor...**

So some say those who are under the law are a slave to the law.

Galatians 4 vs.7 adds;
> **...we are no longer a slave...**

Romans 9:32 also says "pursue by faith not works". Why then would anyone think tithing is still an Old Testament issue when all these verses say it is law and the law has been abolished.

PEOPLE FORGET that the tithe was introduced **way before the law** so it can not be called a law issue and further more the New Testament says we are sons and daughters of Abraham and heirs to the promise.

Galatians 3 vs.29
> **If you are Christ's then are ye Abraham's seed and heirs to The promise**

What promise? The physical blessings Abraham got through faith demonstrated in his actions and his actions included tithing. Does it not surprise some that we quote Abraham's faith yet never care about the way Abraham tithed to prove his faith...?

Tithe because God blessed the first tither Abraham

Since Abraham paid tithe to "Melchizedek king of Salem...the priest of the most high God." Believers are not under the law but they must tithe because Abraham tithed before the law so if it worked for Abraham who is the father of the faith then it will work for me his seed as Galatians 3 vs. 29 says:

Galatians 3 vs. 29
> **If you are Christ's then are ye Abraham's seed and heirs to The promise**

God so blessed Abraham that his servant testified,

Genesis 24 vs.35
> **The LORD hath blessed my master greatly...**

...and it is this blessing we are heirs to that if we do what Abraham did before the law we become partakers of the same blessing. I am not saying that Abraham was blessed solely because he tithed. No, I am not saying that at all. All I am saying was this principle Abraham adopted and later Jacob, worked because it was buried deep in love which is the only law of the believer in this New Covenant.

God blessed him because he was obedient. Since God blessed Abraham for obediently paying tithes WAY BEFORE THE LAW, will He not likewise bless Christians who tithe in obedience to the teachings of the Scriptures?

Tithings Acknowledges God's Ownership of All.

Many years after the death of Abraham God appeared to him in the way, and Jacob surprisingly pledged to tithe and all this way before the law:

Genesis 28 vs.22
...And this stone, which I have set for a pillar, shall be God's house: and of all that thou shalt give me I will surely give thetenth unto thee...

Jacob thus acknowledged God's ownership of all by promising to give to the Lord a tenth of *all*. He promised to tithe because it had worked for his grandfather Abraham and also for his father Isaac. This was a family filled with tithing in their blood and the brilliant thing is love forced them to give. They gave because it was their nature to tithe. We who are Christians are children of love. In cat,

Romans 5 vs.5 says:
The love of God is shed abroad in our hearts by the Holy Spirit

In fact Isaac became rich that;

Genesis 26 vs.14 -15
...he had possession of flocks, and possession of herds, and great store of servants: and the Philistines envied him. For all the wells which his

**father's servants had digged in the days of
Abraham his father, the Philistines
had stopped them, and filled them with earth.**

Isaac was so rich that the whole nation of the *Philistines envied him* they wanted to be him. He followed Abraham's principles and in fact he still possessed some of his father Abraham's wealth and the Philistines even closed some of his riches down yet wherever he went he was rich and could create more wealth just because of obedience created through giving tithing and obedience. The Lord confirmed this in:

Genesis 26 vs. 5;
      **...Abraham obeyed my voice; do thou do so too, and
      the promise shall be sure to thee...**

Abraham's obedience is here celebrated and this is before the law. The argument that tithing is of the law is not supported by scripture at all. It is only supported by those who are stingy and are not real lovers of Christ. Jacob knew he could tithe only if the Lord first gave him something to tithe. Remember God gives the seed to the sower, your job is your seed production centre. It is like a child asking his father for money to buy him a father's Day gift. The money you think is yours has been given you by God and He is simply saying give a tenth and I will increase upon that I have already given you. Jacob acknowledged his father's ownership of all and as believers we MUST do the same.

When Jacob returned to his father's house, God had so blessed him that he:

Genesis 30 vs.43
      **"...had much cattle, and maidservants, and
      menservants, and camels, and asses."**

Christians, too, should tithe to acknowledge God's ownership of all.

Tithe Because God Promised Overflowing Blessings to Tithers.

Malachi 3 vs.10
      **Bring ye all the tithes into the storehouse, that
      there may be meat in mine house, and prove me**

now herewith, saith the LORD of hosts, if I will not open you the windows of heaven, and pour you out a blessing, that there shall not be room enough to receive it."

All the Law of Moses was fulfilled at the cross, but the principle of stewardship, as many other principles, though a part of the law, existed way before the law was given, and remains in effect after the law has been removed. Therefore, the believer should prove God with tithes and offerings, and then claim the blessing God has promised and without tithing the blessing is limited.

Removing tithing because it was in the law is like saying 'I will not believe in worshiping God alone and serving him alone' because that was in the Old Testament. Ceremonial law was removed but tithing was not ceremonial and was established by Abraham way before the law.

Tithe because Jesus tithed and commended tithing.

Contrary to popular belief that Jesus never tithed, Jesus tithed and commended it. So if Jesus tithed I also tithe because he commended it and tithed Himself. He knew the benefits and He knew the principle was for all time and was established way before the law was established.

Remember Jesus commended tithing:

Matthew 23 vs.23

Woe unto you, scribes and Pharisees, hypocrites! For ye pay tithe of mint and anise and cummin, and have omitted the weightier matters of the law, judgment, mercy, and faith: these ought ye to have done, and not to leave the other undone...

Jesus was saying here that, "*You do right to tithe, you do wrong when you leave off judgment, mercy and faith.*"

Tithe because you are commanded to support the Ministry.

If you take care of God's business God will take care of you. Support the work of the Lord and see Him prosper you.

In 1 Corinthians 9:13, Paul reminded Christians that the priests and Levites in Israel lived by the tithes of the people. In the very next verse, he said,

1 Corinthians 9 vs.14
Even so hath the Lord ordained that they which preach the gospel should live of the gospel...

Paul here was writing that those priests of Israel lived by the tithes of the people way back so we ought to understand how to take care of those in ministry. He was saying in effect that just as the priests were given tithes SO shall those that preach the word.

Jesus is the one who receives your tithe not the preacher.

Some do not tithe because they hate the preacher. I remember a certain believer, (if it be right to call people with this mindset believers), who said they will not tithe to their church unless they see the bank statement. Some said they needed a bank account to tithe into. That, my brothers and sisters is not God. That is the devil operating smoothly in the sons of disobedience.

Apostle Paul proved that when you tithe you are not giving to a Pastor though he is the one receiving tithes. Apostle Paul says you are really giving to the Lord Jesus Christ Himself:

Hebrews 7 vs.8
And here men that die receive tithes; but there HE RECEIVETH THEM, of whom it is witnessed that HE LIVETH

The Lord Jesus Christ counts it as paid to Him, personally, for as we have seen:
HE receiveth them...

In **Matthew 25 vs.40** Jesus taught that:
...In as much as ye have done it unto one of the least of These my brethren, ye have done it unto me...

Tithing is a love issue.
If you are not tithing it is only because YOU absolutely have NO LOVE for Christ. It is because you disregard the Lord's work and do not care how the house of the Lord will function. When

you do not tithe you show your level of faith. You expose your unbelief and mistrust directed at God that He will not do anything if you tithe.

As the God of the Old Testament and also the new, Jesus Christ taught tithing. Some do not understand. Jesus Christ *is* the God of the Old Testament.
As the Apostle Paul explained to the:

1 Corinthians 10 vs.1–4:
Moreover, brethren, I do not want you to be unaware That all our fathers were under the cloud, all passed through the sea, all were baptized into Moses in the cloud and in the sea, all ate the same spiritual food, and all drank the same spiritual drink. For they drank of that spiritual Rock that followed them, and that Rock was Christ

Later in this same chapter Apostle Paul wrote:
...Nor let us tempt Christ, as some of them also tempted and were destroyed by serpents...

So it was Christ they were dealing with back in the Old Testament. There are so many references to it and Christ is;

Hebrews 13 vs.8
...the same yesterday, today and forever...

Therefore, no one must not minimize or remove this *fundamental example of tithing* set by the very God we worship. That will be sin and clear disobedience to God. Christians ought to know that if they are not tithing the wealth of the wicked is very far and heaven even far!

However, those who tithe because of the mere fact of obligation will not be blessed for it. They will be missing something in their nature. If these same people change their focus and tithe in love, they will want to help the work of the Lord, expect the Lord to reward them and reach out to lost souls they will be blessed beyond measure.

Should tithing be voluntary?

Tithing should be voluntary in the same way that a man supports his family for BUT AT THE SAME TIME the bible says:

1 Timothy 5 vs.8
> **Any man who does not provide for his own family Is worse than an infidel, they have LOST THEIR FAITH.**

See if tithing is voluntary then the real Christians will do it whilst the not so Christian ones will not. In other words Tithing is a *must* for those who love God. Those who really love God will by nature follow His commandments gladly and cheerfully. See;

John 14 vs.15
> **If you love me, obey my commandments...**

Cheerfulness vs. tithing

Those who love God will not tithe out of compulsion but **out of their nature**. They *will tithe because they love God*! Cheerful giving comes from our nature. Yes God loves a cheerful giver but if the giver is not cheerful that does not mean they need to stop tithing. ALL IT MEANS is they have to change their nature from a sad one to a cheerful one that will make them cheerful givers. 2 Corinthians 9 vs.7 is simply saying we need to get to a point where we give cheerfully out of our cheerful nature that is the point the Holy Spirit is making through Paul.

Remember our nature is a cheerful nature born out of our love for Christ.

Romans 5 vs.5 speaks of our nature;
> **...the love of God is shed abroad in our hearts by the Holy Spirit...**

Now it is no longer a case of acquiring love but acting love out for we already possess the nature of love within us. We cannot pray for love anymore for as believers we were born again with love packaged in the gift of salvation. All we need is to make it abound or in simpler terms to act upon the love we already possess. This is the same with cheerfulness in giving.

Because of the love which was shed abroad in our hearts by the Holy Ghost as Romans 5 vs. 5 says, we are already cheerful people and cheerful givers. What we need now is to act upon the cheerfulness in our hearts when we give. See, it is very simple but people try to run away from it.

2 Corinthians 9 vs.7
God loveth a cheerful giver...

Christians do not need to tithe out of compulsion because if they do they will cease to be Christians and if they do not tithe at all they will also fail to be Christians because a Christian is a person who follows the plans of God and puts God first in their lives. Have you ever wondered that if believers fail to believe that God will provide after giving tithing what on earth are they doing?

Apostle Paul says you must give if you are a believer. You must tithe. See;

1 Corinthians 9 vs.11
If we fed you with spiritual things; is it a big thing if we receive your material things

Jesus believed in tithing

Jesus being God of the Old Testament and the New Testament, taught tithing. Apostle Paul through the Spirit explained to the Corinthian church:

1 Corinthians 10:1–4
Moreover, brethren, I do not want you to be unaware that our fathers were under the cloud, all passed through the sea, all were baptized into Moses in the cloud and in the sea, all ate the same spiritual food, and all drank the same spiritual drink. For they drank of that spiritual Rock that followed them, and that Rock was Christ

In the New Testament we also see the same Apostle Paul proving and adding to the same point by saying:

1 Corinthians 10 vs.9
Nor let us tempt Christ, as some of them also tempted and were destroyed by serpents...

So it was Christ they were dealing with back in the Old Testament just as we are now under Him in the New Testament. There are so many references to the Lordship of Christ both in the Old and the New Testaments.

If you happen to settle this in your heart that:

Hebrews 13:8.
... Christ is the same yesterday, today and forever...
Therefore, we must not refuse or remove this *fundamental principle of tithing* set by the very God we worship. Tithing is an all time principle that is a must for a real believer and real believers do not even ask if it should be done because their very nature makes them cheerful in tithing and offering!

Take care of those God gave you
Take care of the man of God that God has given you and when you give him the blessing will rest in your house. Don't ever think you are enriching the man of God because you can not fully pay him even if you tried.

The anointing upon him is not for his benefit only but for your benefit too. Spiritual things can never be compared to the natural things neither can the natural things be compared to spiritual things. When you get a hold of that principle you will be ready for the 'NOW' wealth.

Chapter Eight
The 'Now' Wealth

Psalm 118 vs.25 says;
**Save Now, I beseech thee, Oh Lord, Oh Lord,
I beseech Thee, send Now Prosperity.**

Let every fibre of your being, every pore on your body and every cell of your blood soak into the reality that God deals in the 'Now' and lives in a 'One eternal Now'. He can not answer your prayers tomorrow for He does not have a tomorrow to answer your prayers in. God does not have a yesterday. He is not governed by time. He is into the 'Now' prosperity!

He does not sleep so He does not have a tomorrow. He has never slept so He can not have a yesterday. To God everything is seen today, even the thing that shall happen in our tomorrow God sees that thing as if it is already so. He lives in 'one eternal NOW' so the wealth of the wicked can be obtained NOW and not later.

As aforementioned God lives in 'one eternal now' so He requires us to use that faith to take over the wealth of the wicked today and not tomorrow. That is why the word says:

Hebrews 11 vs.1
**NOW FAITH IS the substance of things hoped for,
the evidence of things not seen**

The scripture does not say "TOMORROW faith will be..." It does not say "YESTERDAY faith was..." BUT IT SAYS...

"NOW FAITH IS"

...so when you get to the truth of taking over the wealth of the wicked you need to believe in God bringing your wealth today FOR faith is 'NOW'. That is why the bible says:

Mark,11vs.24
**Therefore I say to you, whatever things you ask
when you pray, believe that you receive them, and
you will have them.**

The receiving of the wealth is supposed to be now and not tomorrow but the having might come later - maybe two minutes later or two months later or a year later or whatever the time but the receiving of the wealth of the wicked- the 'lambano' of it has to be "when you pray" not after you pray, but whilst you pray:

...believe you receive and you shall...

The greatest wealth transfer is Now

When you believe you receive whilst praying, not after you pray but whilst you are praying, you will have thrust a faith seed into your future so that when you reach that future you will find it in a multiplied state. God has already shown us that He accepts a 'now' wealth.

Psalm 118 vs.25
...Save, Oh Lord send Now Prosperity...

The book of Psalm got the picture and the scripture declares that prosperity has to be sent NOW. It is not for tomorrow. It is for now.

NOW means NOW.

Now many believers have become too spiritually minded, which is good, but in their too spiritually minded state they have become no earthly good. They just want to enjoy God with their hands lifted up and some with plenty of tongues yet the demonstration of that gospel is nowhere to be found. That is why sinners think believers are crazy. They look at believers who have taken a poverty vow and they never want to be Christians. What is in the word does not match up to the poverty some believers are in. The disease can also be a simple one - POSTPONING their blessing.

They have not taken the 'now' of God to mean 'now'. To believers, faith works by love and love needs patience - that is scriptural - BUT - believers have taken the word *patience* to mean; years waiting, whereas to God it means 'anytime from now'.

However God is not in the mafia, God is not a joker. He wants His children to have plenty, but to be able to do that believers need to run away from this mindset. They need to understand the power of THE NOW WEALTH and the power of what they already possess so that all that they have so far will not go to waste. The 'NOW' wealth should be obtained by what one has right 'now'

The power of what you already possess

The question in your mind is "Where do I start? I do not have enough money" God's answer is "Money is not your problem. Faith is." When you understand faith you will understand that what you have now will guarantee you what you do not have.

Look at David's story before we go any further;

Judges 20 vs.16
> **Among all this people there were seven hundred chosen men left handed: every one could sling stones at an hair breath, and not miss.**

Among the Israelite army were seven hundred skilled men who could shoot a stone at hair's breath and not miss but they were so confused and frightened by the size of their problem (Goliath) that they cowered when they saw him, their knees buckled, their pants did not, their legs trembled before him and their stone quivers rattled with fear.

The scriptures say these men literally ran in fear of this giant pagan yet David dared to be unique. He was pushed by a revelation far different from the rest of the Israelite army. He wanted the wealth of the wicked to belong to Israel.

I Samuel 17 vs.49-50 says:
> **...David put his hand in his bag and took thence a stone, and slang it, and smote the Philistine in his forehead, that the stone sunk in his forehead; and fell, upon his face...so David prevailed over the Philistine with a sling and with a stone...and there was no sword in the hand of David...**

The biggest mistake brewed by many believers who profess that the stone David used to kill Goliath was Holy Ghost guided is a great escape from the reality. It is the longest way of saying nothing for those who love to speak and utter the evidently unscriptural. It is in a sense a denial of that which God being God has embedded within human beings, His creatures.

Notice, the Holy Spirit is always involved in what we do if we are really believers but here the stone was not only a result of the Holy Spirit guiding but of another level the Holy Ghost had made David to reach.

David however knew that his skill for killing Goliath came from his history in killing a lion and a bear. He simply says it was the practise that made him a victor. This practice was led by the Holy Spirit. He said it was what the Holy Ghost had trained him to do way before this uncircumcised Goliath showed up that made the difference. In short, what David had gave him what he did not have.

Although the practise was provided by God, David did not deny or hide the fact that God has a way of preparing His people for future events. David used what God gave him way before the time of his encounter with this uncircumcised Philistine by the name Goliath. David was now using what He already had to obtain what He did not have. Even though you might not know it, there is something that the Lord gave you which can be used to take over the wealth of the wicked. Find it out and use it. See!

Your destiny lies in your ability to find what God has blessed you with, develop it through encounters with the lion and bears of many projects - because if you do not, you will spend too much time praying to God to give you what He has already given you.

Do not wait until you have a bright idea, get ready getting the wealth of the wicked now using what you already have and when the bright idea comes it will find you on your way to your wealthy place. If you wait for a bright idea it might take years to come and when it arrives you will have a few resources to tackle it. That will get you disappointed and discouraged. Use what you have, no matter how small, to obtain what you do not have.

Using what you have

Apostle Paul says:

Ephesians 5 vs.1
...Be ye imitators of God...

So we follow God's example. When God wanted Eve, He used what He had and what He Had was Adam. He made Adam to take a deep sleep and from Adam's rib brought him a wife, Eve. This is a sign for us believers to understand that all the things we desire are right inside us, wrapped in who we are.

The billions you need are right inside of you, wrapped inside you by God Himself. What you have will bring you what you do not have just as Adam produced Eve through God. We are carriers of the divine nature;

2 Peter 1 vs.4 says:
...partakers of the divine nature...

Scripture adds:

2 Corinthians 4 vs.7
We have this treasure in earthen vessels...

In David's case, he knew the first time he had an encounter with the lion that it was God's fingerprint to what was to follow. Whilst it is the Holy Ghost of God that guides you, the reality is what that same Holy Spirit gives you will still remain within you even if you deviate from the way hence:

Romans 11 vs. 29
...gifts and callings of the Lord are without repentance...

The Holy Spirit being God, will not take away what He gave you but when you miss the point of contact then your gift stays dormant until you have in yourself a renewed person or is then used for the devil's purposes. One of the gifts David so much possessed was the ability and agility to move with the vision and to spot opportunities.

David's experience

Have you ever researched on what the armour of the Philistines or the Israelites' for that matter was like in those days? Every time a warrior threw his head backwards the head covering opened to reveal the formerly obscured eyebrows and fearsome forehead of a warrior. Many warriors in the day and age of David used this tactic to intimidate their opponents by the sheer ugliness and apparently fearless faces.

When Goliath thought of throwing his head backwards to expose his hideous forehead, David saw an opportunity and shot right in the middle of his forehead. Goliath was dead just because David knew the reality of spotting an opportunity. God gave him that ability and he employed it.

Whilst our Lord Jesus Christ is our guide, I only used David since he represents in this instance a person thought lowly of. His own father forgot about him when the prophet Samuel came in search of the one to be king. Samuel himself thought one of his brothers was the one instead of David. His own father made him heard sheep alone in the thickets of the bushes. His brothers made jokes of him and thought of him mad and a show off when he dared confront Goliath. This can happen to you or is happening to you. People might not believe in you but when you know you are called you ought to do what God tells you to do without listening to critics if you are really serious about taking over the wealth of the wicked.

David knew that what he possessed was far more than any man could convince him otherwise. He was made fun of, ridiculed and thought of as mad but it did not stop him from pursuing his goal and putting to use what God had placed in him during his days as a shepherd. He was well aware of God's calling in his life and he was ready to follow it.

That reminds me of the time we started talking about building a range of supermarkets in a certain country. Many thought we were crazy yet we knew the revelation on taking over the wealth of the wicked that we were not bored by the criticism. We kept our confession amidst opposition and you guessed it those people were the first to claim they always knew we could do it when we began the purchasing of land. We knew our call along the wealth route and we followed it.

David knew his call: the call to kill Goliath and this pagan Goliath knew his call: the call to die miserably!

Moses' rod

God asked Moses, "What do you have?" and Moses answered, "A stick"; and God thought of using that stick to turn into a snake.

It is the same rod that brought forth water out of a rock. What Moses had, brought the snake he did not have. What Moses had, brought the water the children of Israel did not have.

In order to take the wealth of the wicked - it does not matter how much you have, *for what you have will get you to where you never thought you could get.*

It is the same with the widow's oil, she had no money to pay off her debtors but when she approached the man of God with her problem, the jar of oil she had turned into many jars. With what she had brought forth she never thought she would get.

Getting to having what you do not have

Remember Ezekiel's dry bones, in the Valley of Dry Bones. Ezekiel receives a word to prophesy to the dry bones after he first had a burning desire to speak to God. Within half of no time God tells him to speak to the dry bones and make flesh come to them. What Ezekiel had was a mouth that could utter words. He had no money but still God showed Him "Money was not the problem; only faith can be a hindrance if it is not there"

Notice, flesh really came to the bones when Ezekiel spoke but the breath had not and God had to tell him to prophesy to the breath.

If Ezekiel had ended at the flesh coming to the bones then the miracle would simply have been incomplete, it is as simple to understand as that.

In your way to having what you do not have God expects you to be obedient and follow every step, one step at a time for him to get you to reach *the wealth of the wicked.*

Your lack of wealth shall bow to God

The Bible says Goliath fell face down after the sling shot hit him on the forehead, all because of what David already possessed. It is scientifically senseless to fall face down after being engulfed by a pain that is forcefully going backwards and in such a force that would cause someone as large as Goliath to die.

A closer look shows that when God gives you a breakthrough it tears to pieces, shreds and burns to ashes all points of reason. By

Goliath falling face down, Goliath in his entire blasphemous mouth acknowledged the power of the sovereign God. That is why the bible says:

Hebrews 11 vs.1
Now faith is...

Not "Now sense is..." for faith does not have to make sense. It only has to make faith. Faith does not need to explain itself. It simply wins. It makes a giant out of a wimp and a possessor out of a lack. Every time you see faith in the word there is possessing of wealth and power.

See this;

...To them that believed GAVE HE POWER...

...Whosoever believes in Him...have eternal life...

...become partakers of the divine nature...

See what **Hebrews 11** says;
By faith he was commended as a righteous man, when God spoke well of his offerings. And by faith he still speaks, even though he is dead...

By faith Enoch was taken from this life, so that he did not experience death; he could not be found, because God had taken him away. For before he was taken, he was commended as one who pleased God...

By faith Noah, when warned about things not yet seen, in holy fear built an ark to save his family. By his faith he condemned the world and became heir of the righteousness that comes by faith...

By faith Abraham, when called to go to a place he would later receive as his inheritance, obeyed and went, even though he did not know where he was going...

By faith he made his home in the Promised Land like a stranger in a foreign country; he lived in tents, as did Isaac and Jacob, who were heirs with him of the same promise...

By faith Abraham, even though he was past age— and Sarah herself was barren—was enabled to become a father because he considered him faithful who had made the promise...

Plus many more verses that prove this point.

When you have faith you have what is needed to obtain what you do not have. However, never forget why you become a possessor. You become a wealth magnate so as to finance the work of God, and do not get me wrong. When I say to finance the work of God I am not advocating that you spend your money on a hungry and greedy preacher who tells you if you send him some money you will be blessed by his anointing.

Have you ever asked why those preachers do not send you money so they can be blessed too like they want you to be blessed when you send them money. This wealth is not to wolves in sheep's clothing. The wealth which is already inside you is to finance the real gospel. Preachers are part of the gospel but preachers should never use the people of God and in turn the people of God should continuously give to God without fear that the preacher will cheat them.

Remember to get the 'HOW' out of your life.

It is high time believers stop asking how they are going to do it, and realise that what they have will get them what they do not have.

The billions you need are right inside of you, wrapped inside you by God Himself. What you have will bring you what you do not have just as Adam produced Eve through God. We are carriers of the divine nature. We can produce by faith what we do not have. All we need is faith. We need to act upon what we believe and that acting upon the word of God that we believe in will get us what we do not have.

Remember revelation is not the truth you know, *it is the truth you use* so use this truth and see the kingdom advance to new heights. Now, what is needed is that your time to shine as a wealth magnet can come through a person or a vessel you undermine. It can come through a brother you believe is really low spiritually or think is under you concerning the things of the Spirit but be warned that same brother or sister might be the vessel God chooses. This might not make sense but it sure makes faith!

Faith makes faith and not sense

Look at how it came to Namaan:

2 Kings 5 vs.10
> **And Elisha sent a messenger unto him saying, Go and wash in Jordan seven times, and thy flesh shall come again to thee and thou shalt be clean**

The glow of the Jordan River with its muddy waters disgusted Naaman. Even Elisha's messenger gave Naaman a lack of options and God Himself seemed to have ignored Namaan's feel of superiority. He was a suffering man full of pain from leprosy but he thought lowly of God's command. He became comfortable with his leprosy than in the remedy of washing himself clean in the muddy water of the Jordan River.

Why God did not choose the waters of Abana and Pharpa which were a lot cleaner troubled him:
> **Are not Abana and Pharpa rivers of Damascus better than all the waters of Israel? May I not wash in them and be clean? So he turned and went away in a rage**

Namaan could not contain it. The word of God seemed to strip off him the shells of his seniority complex. In the midst of all this, his healing could only come by way of these dirty waters of Jordan. Namaan was torn apart and decided to leave. It was his idea that if God could heal him, the least he could do was do what to him seemed intellectual, and that was bathing him in Abana and Pharpa, the cleaner rivers as compared to the suggested Jordan. The scriptures give us a word of warning:

Let no man think highly of himself more than he ought to lest he fall

Namaan thought of Himself more than he ought to. He wanted his way not God's way. He wanted God to show respect instead God tells Elisha not to even meet Namaan but to send a servant to deliver the message:

2 Kings 5 vs.10

Go and wash in Jordan seven times, and thy flesh shall come again to thee and thou shalt be clean

A difference of taste between an uncompromising, infinite God and a finite Captain with leprosy for that matter became a problem. The infinite God is in heaven, clean, holy and alive, no leprosy in sight. Namaan, the captain was wondering in his weary world, his body swamped by leprosy. There was no one to help him with the exception of this servant of the man of God who kept pointing his forefinger towards the muddy waters of Jordan. Namaan's servants though afraid of the disease lingered around with tremors in their voices convincing Namaan to listern to Elisha.

2 Kings 5 vs.14

Then went he down, and dipped himself seven times in Jordan, according to the saying of the man of God: and his flesh came again like unto the flesh of a little child and he was clean.

Whatever God says is to be followed without a shadow of doubt. This is a place where we cannot weigh the pros and cons of what God has instructed but where only the pros and the many illogical instructions are trusted so as to obtain the occurrences of the improbable and get the wealth of the wicked. It does not matter who brings it to us because many times God uses the *"foolish to confound the wise"*. *Sometimes God gives you what you take as a foolish command and he expects you to follow it no matter the case.*

Disobedience in my life

When I held the first prophetic summit in the city of Manchester United Kingdom, I heard God say to me call out the name of a deaf person and the deaf ear will open. I started to debate within myself on why I should call out that name. I thought if the man was deaf he would not hear me anyway so I will not intimidate myself with what God is trying to do. I kept on calling out cases and names of people I did not know as God gave them to me but when I got to calling out another case, using the word of knowledge and discerning of spirits, which involved suicide, I suddenly felt that the anointing was lifting off of me. I had entered in to disobedience by not calling out that case.

I knew the anointing was now lifting for that day and began to repent. God was merciful without even calling out the name the man came forward pointing and touching his ears indicating that He could not hear and that he wanted God to heal him. I placed my hands into his ears and he received a miracle. Unto this day He is well but my disobedience could have cost me and that man's hearing.

Obedience in wealth

Many a time God's instructions sound, seem and are counted among the "foolish" things on this earth by those who have failed to understand that faith does not have to make sense. They have looked at the word of God, the dysfunctional areas of this world, the diseases and poverty on the earth and concluded that what God says is merely fiction- if not foolish or is simply spiritual and cannot be put into practice here on earth. They have spiritualised everything but obedience is essential.

Follow instructions

Take God's instructions no matter how hard they are, for in them is power to obtain what we do not have. Think of God instructing Moses to lift a handful of ground loam then turning it into mosquitoes. What of five loaves feeding thousands. What about a stick turning into a snake. Can I take you to Hosea being instructed to marry a prostitute just to fulfil God's own theological needs? Let us talk of Moses, old as he was, being instructed to raise a rod so as to give the Israelites victory in the war being fought in the valley.

What of Isaiah preaching naked for three years at God's command. Let us come back to the story of Namaan being told to wash his unclean leprosy in the unclean waters of the Jordan. You might agree with Elisha for surely what happened to the cleaner waters of Abana and Pharpa? Is there a bunch of holy tablets within the Jordan? No, but God just prefered the dirty waters to the cleaner ones.

God Himself shows no sign of concern or anger through all those ridiculous suggestions by His creatures. No wonder the Bible says:

1 Corinthians 1 vs.25
> **...the foolishness of God is wiser than men; and the weakness of God stronger than men.**

That which seems to be stupidity to many is nothing less than God's uncompromising path to "...destroy the wisdom of the wise, and...bring to nothing the understanding of the prudent". It is in these seemingly stupid commands of God that our destiny is shaped and through this we are able to take over the wealth of the wicked. God's main concern is to demolish the understanding of the prudent and blind those who say they can see. Paul asks:

1 Corinthians 1 vs.20-21
> **Where is the wise? Where is the scribe? Where is the disputer of this world? Hath not God made foolish the wisdom of this world? For after that in the wisdom of God the world by wisdom knew not God, it pleased God by foolishness...to save them that believe**

God chooses who he wants
When a certain man saw an angel behind me in my church he went and commented about the anointing in our ministry to which this preacher who was being told answered in a way that showed disbelief. Many who knew about my calling simply could not believe God would speak to me. Now many do because they have seen more than they thought but still some ascribe it to the devil and some simply do not know. Their question is mainly "why you?" but I have a question "why not me?"

Namaan might have laughed out of his socks, if he had any that is, when the good news of his survival was delivered not only from a little girl but from a captive little girl. Couldn't God have found better people to deliver His word to the captain? To him it was a little bit insensible for God to talk through a small girl He (God) could not protect when they took her captive but God does what He sees best. Paul adds:

1 Corinthians 1 vs.26-27
> **For ye see your calling brethren, how that not wise men after the flesh, not many might, not many noble, are called: but God hath chosen the foolish things of the world to confound the...wise; and God hath chosen the weak things of the world to confound the things which are mighty...**

When we were told by God to start Spirit Embassy, people never expected God to do what He began to do in our ministry. Many times I'll be standing in church and I see visions of what people where doing in their houses and hear what they were saying. By the Spirit of God I am able to mention names of places and people I have never seen or heard of.

Many people did not expect that from me yet God chose me anyway. I also did not expect it more than I expected to be the first man to land on the moon. The bible simply says:

1 Corinthians 1 vs.25
> **...the foolishness of God is wiser than men; and the weakness of God stronger than men.**

When we say "it can not be" God says "It can be"

Many times God will make you meet the least expected person who will offer you a crazy strategy to get your breakthrough at the time you may wish to speak to what every mortal calls the epitome of faith. Follow the commands, do not classify people or put them into groups. Quit being God. The truth is God will demolish all of your predicaments if you quit begging for the power that you already have and stop voting on what He has already commanded you to do or who he has already sent to you!

Do Not argue with God.

A certain story is told of a mountain climber who slipped from the summit of Mount Everest only to hang in the air supported by his climbing rope. In his peril, the climber cried out to God for help: "Is there a God out there?" The climber cried out and the Lord answered the climber.

"I am here my son"
Tell me what to do in my predicament Lord" the climber begged.
"Let go of the rope that supports you" came God's response. Seeing and perceiving God's response as a hard nut to crack and an absolute impossibility the climber cried again in the gloom of the night.
"Is there another God out there with a different idea
to that of the one who said 'let go of the rope'?" In the silent came a reply from the one God that had previously answered him.
"My son there is no other God beside me and I am telling you again to let go of the rope before it is too late"
"Is there another option my Lord?"
"None my son, only let go of the rope and it will all be well. If you do not want to obey I am off, I do not have time for those who do not obey"

The climber refused to let go and as a result he was found dead the next morning by other climbers but surprisingly enough, *his body was just twenty centimetres from the ground,* so when God said let go of the rope, He knew the distance the climber was from the ground would not kill him if he had let go.

There are many things in life that God tells us to take up, live or throw away and in many cases it would seem for a moment that His commands are vain and ill thought but we are called to follow them any way if we are to overcome the evil of poverty or sickness. We should quit voting on what God tells us to do. Quit voting now and watch God do greater things in your life. Quit arguing with God and watch the wealth of the wicked answering the door when you knock.

Papa Kenneth Hagin wrote in his Bible that "My Bible says it I believe it and that settles it." That is a great statement and good stance for all believers to take for if the bible says it we have to believe in what it says and act upon it irregardless of whether we feel like it or not if we are ever going to take over the wealth of the wicked.

In my bible I also wrote "My Bible says it, I believe it, I act upon it and that settles it" See!

If God says to do something I will obey and when I obey, what I have will guarantee me what I do not have. That cancels the question "Where do I start? I do not have enough money."

Chapter Nine
Only Believe

God's Miraculous Provision for Samaria

The cure of 'Doubt' is 'Doubt'!

'Doubt' can cure 'doubt' more than anything can. "Should it not be faith that cures doubt?" You may ask.

Doubting your doubts

The reason is 'doubt' if directed at the devil is good and is faith. When you doubt your 'doubts' you will have entered into faith for doubts doubted cease to be doubts but become faith. Whenever doubt pours in, doubt that doubt.

If the devil sends doubt to you by saying "you will never finance the kingdom by the wealth of the wicked" just turn to him and doubt what he says. When you doubt the devil you enter into the realm of faith. See!

The devil needs to be doubted. So many believers are suffering from doubt problems yet they can use that doubt to turn the tide in their favor. You can use your doubt not to doubt God but to doubt the devil and when you do, the devil will not be able to stand it. He will leave for he can not stand to be doubted.

He can come to you and tell you "this wealth thing is of the devil" just turn and face him - tell him "I doubt you with everything in me - I choose to follow what God says and I choose to doubt the devil".

Doubting God will kill you but doubting the devil always will preserve you.

In the days the Syrian army surrounded the walls of Samaria, the city and all the people could not get out of the gates to find food or water. They were starving and if they thought of going outside they would die at the hands of the Syrians. In fact the situation became too hard that they started to eat:

2 Kings 6 vs.25
...dove's dung...
In the nick of time God spoke to His servant Elisha and said:

2 Kings 7 vs.1
Hear the word of the Lord. Thus says the Lord: 'Tomorrow about this time a seah of fine flour shall be sold for a shekel, and two seahs of barley for a shekel, at the gate of Samaria.

However, an officer on whose hand the king leaned got into doubt - doubted the word of God instead of the devil - and answered the man of God and said,

Look, *if* the LORD would make windows in heaven, could this thing be?

And the man of God answered the officer,

In fact, you shall see *it* with your eyes, but you shall not eat of it.

Doubting God on issues that he makes plain in his word will make you;

...see *it* with your eyes, but you shall not eat of it...

When the revelation of wealth comes to you and every fiber of your being starts using it, do not entertain doubting the Lord. It does not matter how hard it is to believe. Elisha believed God even when the circumstances were hard. People would eat each other's children due to the hunger that was upon Samaria. It was unbearable, but God specializes in the unbearable. Remember the scripture that says:

Philippians 4 vs.19
My God shall supply all your needs...

Hard to believe

By the standards of that time, the prices listed were not cheap; but they were nothing compared to the famine conditions that come upon as a result of the siege of Samaria. The prices the prophet spoke of were way better though not cheap. The man of God prophesied that by the next day conditions would so improve that good products would be available again, even though at a substantial price and that was still unbelievable to some. It was hard to believe and unbelief can not take over the wealth of the wicked.

Facts of the miracle

...Hear the word of the LORD...

Though the King of Israel blamed the LORD for the calamity that came upon Israel and Samaria, God still had a word for the king and the nation and this word was not a good word yet God wanted it heard. Some did not want to hear it; they were doubting the Lord instead of doubting the devil who had spoken through the King's officer.

...Tomorrow about this time...

God's promise through Elisha was that in 24 hours the economic situation in Samaria would be completely reversed through a miracle. Instead of scarcity, there would be such abundance that food prices would radically drop in the city. That is a 24 hour miracle that anyone can obtain!

How they doubted God and not the devil

Look, if the Lord would make windows in heaven, could this thing be?

The king's officer doubted the prophecy, and his doubt was based on several faulty grounds. The past for him dictated the future. He was still in the past when God was thinking of the future. Doubting God clouded his eyes just as it will cloud your power to take over the wealth of the wicked.

We should never doubt God. We are born into His good family. Doubting God should never become part of us. We should however become one with the word to the extent that when circumstances come to us and squeeze us - all that comes out is the juice of the word - word juice.

Now, the first thing the officer of the King doubted was the *power* of God, yet if God willed it, He certainly could make windows in heaven and drop down food from the sky for the hungry, besieged city of Samaria; but God meant another way.

Second, he doubted the *way* God wanted to bring about the miracle. In the mind of the king's officer, the 'modus operandi' (way of doing things) of God was not real. He took it too literally because he was trying to calculate the *chemical composition of this miracle.*

He had no idea that God could bring provision in a completely unexpected way.

Third, he doubted the *messenger* of God. Though the promise was admittedly hard to believe, the king's officer could have and should have believed it because it came from a man with an established track record of reliability. In fact even without this the officer could have believed if he knew like he did that Elisha was a Prophet for the word of God says;

2 Chronicles 20 vs.20
   ...Believe His prophets and so shall you prosper...

Notice the steps the officer took in doubting God. Doubt dared to question the truthfulness of God's promise itself. Understand this, your ability to take over the wealth of the wicked ends where doubt's question mark starts.

Doubt's voice said, "This is a *new* thing and cannot be true."
Doubt's voice said, "This is a *sudden* thing and cannot be true."
Doubt's voice said, "There is no way to accomplish this thing."
Doubt's voice said, "There is only one way God can work."
Doubt's voice said, "Even if God does something, it won't be enough."

The prophet was not fazed. He believed the word of God. He took the stance "If God says it I believe it, I act upon it and that settles it". Elisha was one with the word of God.
The Devil could not make him doubt God. He simply replied the officer's unbelief with another prophecy.

**...In fact, you shall see it with your eyes,
   but you shall not eat of it...**

God pronounced judgment upon the king's doubting officer through His Servant Elisha. He would see the word fulfilled, but not benefit from its fulfillment. The wages of doubt which is sin was still death and the officer of the king would see it but die without benefiting from it.

The wealth coming forth

The wealth that Elisha pronounced from God was to come upon every person except the unbelievers. That is exactly what will happen with this revelation of talking over the wealth of the wicked. It is not something that is coming - some have already used it and have used their wealth for the kingdom. They are also some that have left their true love because of it but that should not stop us from acquiring it for the purpose of the Gospel. What Elisha said is exactly supported by; Apostle Paul who says:

Hebrews 12 vs. 22
...We are come unto mount Zion...

And Isaiah who adds by saying, in Mount Zion;

Isaiah 33 vs. 23 and 35 vs. 6
...Even the lame take the prey...the lame man
Leap like an hart...

If the lame believes, he or she will take the prey. If those without wealth believe, they will also take up wealth to use for Godly purposes. It is money with a mission. Only believe all things are possible and amaze the world as you win souls without money being an option.

See what lepers did in that day

Now there were four leprous men at the entrance of the gate; and they said to one another,
> **"Why are we sitting here until we die? If we say, 'We will enter the city,' the famine is in the city, and we shall die there. And if we sit here, we die also. Now therefore, come, let us surrender to the army of the Syrians. If they keep us alive, we shall live; and if they kill us, we shall only die." And they rose at twilight to go to the camp of the Syrians; and**

when they had come to the outskirts of the Syrian camp, to their surprise no one was there.

These men stayed at the entrance of the gate because they were not welcome in the city. This is another example of not choosing who will bring your miracle. In fact Jeremiah 3 vs. 15 says;

I will send you pastors after my own heart...

God is the one who chooses who brings your miracle. By so saying I am not saying we should not choose those who should be around us. On the contrary we should; because the word says we should be around those who love him and it is these people we should not choose from when it comes to who God will choose to bring a miracle through.

Now back to the leprous men. Their leprous condition made them outcasts and untouchables. They were just like some today who believe this wealth is for a few and their situation can not catapult them into their wealthy place BUT they possessed a little bit more - Hope - a *goal setter* and when they decided to go out and look for food - faith came in - *a goal getter.*

The common sense

2 Kings 7 vs.3-6

Why sit we here until we die? If we say, We will enter into the city, then the famine is in the city, and we shall die there: and if we sit still here, we die also. Now therefore come, and let us fall unto the host of the Syrians: if they save us alive, we shall live; and if they kill us, we shall but die. And they rose up in the twilight, to go unto the camp of the Syrians: and when they were come to the uttermost part of the camp of Syria, behold, there was no man there.
For the LORD had made the host of the Syrians to hear a noise of chariots, and a noise of horses, even the noise of a great host: and they said one to another, Lo, the king of Israel hath hired against us the kings of the Hittites, and the kings of the Egyptians, to come upon us.

Spurgeon said "Now you perceive that there are just two courses open to you; you can sit still, but then you know that you must perish; or you can go to Christ, and your fear is that you will perish then. Yet you can but die if you go to him, and he rejects you; whereas, if you do not go to him, you must surely perish" **The miracle takes shape.**

When the four lepers came to the outskirts of the Syrian camp the bible says, **to their surprise no one was there**

Verse 8 says;
> **And when these lepers came to the uttermost part of the camp, they went into one tent, and did eat and drink, and carried thence silver, and gold, and raiment, and went and hid it; and came again, and entered into another tent, and carried thence also, and went and hid it.**

The huge army which surrounded the city of Samaria for many months until people started eating dove's dung, their own children and was the home and supply center for thousands of men. When the lepers came upon it that morning, they discovered an empty army camp – fully supplied, but empty of men.

The words, to the outskirts of the Syrian camp imply that they came not only to the edge of the camp, but that they walked around to the furthest part of the Syrian camp, the part away from the city. They came to the camp as someone from afar would approach, not as someone from Syria. They figured that this was their best chance, coming as if they were not from the besieged city and to the least fortified positions of the camp. This was however a plan by the Holy Spirit.

Did the Lord in some way magnify the stumbling footsteps of the lepers as they made their way around the camp's opposite end and the Syrian heard a noise of chariots? No, He did not – I believe chariots of fire surrounded them like they did Elijah and his servant. What the Syrian army heard was a sound of horses and chariots from another world - the spiritual realm. An army from heaven itself!

How God did it

The LORD had caused the army of the Syrians to hear the noise of chariots and the noise of horses; the noise of a great army; so they said to one another;

2 Kings 7 vs.6
Look, the king of Israel has hired against us the kings of the Hittites and the kings of the Egyptians to attack us!" Therefore they arose and fled at twilight, and left the camp intact; their tents, their horses, and their donkeys; and they fled for their lives...

Israel was powerless against this besieging army, but God wasn't powerless. God had a power to make them hear the sound of a great army. This was not an illusion. God really sent an army of a *different species* but He attacked the Syrian army simply by causing them to *hear* the *noise* of an army.

For the LORD had caused the army of the Syrians to hear the noise of chariots . . . the noise of a great army

Whether one believes God did this by putting the noise into the air or by simply creating the illusion of the noise in the minds of the Syrian soldiers - that does not matter one little bit. What matters is God did it, it happened and He can do the same today if you dare believe wealth can come to you for the purpose of the Gospel. The same God who struck one Syrian army so they could not see what *was* there can now strike your poverty so it can hear things that *are not seen and hear an abundance of wealth coming your way.*

Your poverty or your lack of wealth shall hear a sound of an army and your poverty shall flee leaving riches in its place. Your bill shall hear a sound of money coming to pay it and it will flee leaving a paid bill. You only need to believe that all things are possible. The Syrian Army left everything behind, leaving the unlikely lepers to spoil the camp. It became the plundering of the Syrians. Favor over matter!

As a result, *the siege for Samaria was over* – even though no one in the city *knew* it or *enjoyed* it. They were as free as the harts of the wilderness had they known it: but their ignorance held them in poverty. Ignorance like doubt which comes from the same thing can keep you to enjoy life and be in health as thy soul prospers.

When wealth comes you have a responsibility.

The church today has seen too many superstar preachers whose main aim is to buy jets, cars, mansions and all the latest gadgets to show they have made it in the ministry. Now I am not saying it is wrong to use these things for the work before us but our aim should not be to show off or be extravagant like many are doing today. It is with these same preachers that you get scandal after scandal.

They will make you fill in a form mentioning how many people you have if you call them to preach in your church. In fact I know a man who literally demanded to a preacher who had invited him that he wanted the most expensive hotel in town. Now, don't get me wrong - I am also a man of God and I believe in taking good care of God's servants, but we should not be demanding. At the same time we should learn to treat man of God better than anyone here on earth for they watch over our souls as the word says.

Now if Apostle Paul was here he would puke at these men and women's behavior. They have lost the plot. They think of filling their bellies and not helping other ministries grow.

However, when these lepers came to the outskirts of the camp, they went into one tent and ate and drank, and carried from it silver and gold and clothing, and went and hid *them;* then they came back and entered another tent, and carried *some* from there *also,* and went and hid *it.* Then they remembered those in the gates - the same people who saw them as outcasts - and they said to one another;

2 Kings 7 vs. 9
> **We are not doing right. This day is a day of good news, and we remain silent. If we wait until morning light, some punishment will come upon us. Now therefore, come, let us go and tell the king's household...**

The lepers rightly enjoyed the miracle God provided but they also realized that the gift God gave them had a responsibility attached to it which was to share it with others. They understood that to remain silent and to selfishly enjoy their blessings on their own would be sin. They had a responsibility to share the good news. You as a believer, have the duty to inform others on how to *lambano* the wealth of the wicked for Godly purposes. When you carry out your duties - believers will start calling out the shots in many areas of life. The greatest wealth transfer will happen so quick the devil will be caught unawares.

Surely, Jesus did not come to save us that we might live unto ourselves. He came to save us from selfishness. He came to save us even from ourselves so that when the wealth of the wicked comes it will be used for God's work and not for selfish purposes.

Before the prophecy came to pass.

The bible tells us that the lepers went to the gatekeepers of the city (notice they were still lepers not allowed to enter), and told them, saying,

> ...We went to the Syrian camp, and surprisingly no one was there, not a human sound; only horses and donkeys tied, and the tents intact." And the gatekeepers called out, and they told it to the king's household inside. So the king arose in the night and said to his servants, "Let me now tell you what the Syrians have done to us. They know that we are hungry; therefore they have gone out of the camp to hide themselves in the field, saying, 'When they come out of the city, we shall catch them alive, and get into the city...

The king was still in unbelief!

And one of his servants answered and said, *"Please, let several men take five of the remaining horses which are left in the city. Look, they may either become like all the multitude of Israel that are left in it; or indeed, I say, they may become like all the multitude of Israel left from those who are consumed; so let us send them and see."* Therefore they took two chariots with horses; and the king sent them in the direction of the Syrian army, saying, *"Go and see."* And they went after them to the Jordan; and indeed all the road *was* full of garments and weapons which the Syrians had thrown away in their haste. So the messengers returned and told the king.

Despising the messenger of God

Since the lepers were not allowed in the city because they were regarded unclean, they could only communicate with the gatekeepers. Remember that your miracle might come with those you do not expect. However those who do not despise their message bearer will obtain the promises of God. They will be very near to receiving the wealth of the wicked.

These lepers had many people they were not allowed to speak to, but they were faithful to speak to the ones whom they *could* speak to. If you see yourself being despised - deliver the message through another way. Those who take it will benefit but those who do not will lose out.

Error in believers

I remember when the church of a certain man who showed(s) miracles on TV came to our town, many *babes* in Christ left their good churches to be in that man's church. In their scores they left where God had planted them simply because they believed that that man had all the answers to life. They liked the buzz of being associated with the man but God was not smiling.

So is the mind of children in the things of the Spirit - they despise where God has put them. They sign off their future and follow after the wind and when that bubble bursts it will be too late to find a way out. It was not long until the people in that church started thinking their man of God was "the way". They turned a good church into a cult and those people are in it without realizing it.

The problem is that today rebuking a believer is chasing them away. Believers are not taking rebuke for disobedience and Pastors are afraid to lose people so they better not rebuke them because when you rebuke them they run away and find another church. Many have too many ideas that have no place or that do not give any place for God's views and when you correct them they leave you church or simply resign from what you sent them to do.

In my church I used to have people like this and I know I will have them many times over but I am for God's work and I fear no man. I will rebuke and will not follow their views if those views do not line up with the word. I work for God and not for men.

God had already given a warning:
2 Timothy 4 vs.2-4
> **Preach the word; be instant in season, out of season; reprove, rebuke, exhort with all longsuffering and doctrine.**
> **For the time will come when they will not endure sound doctrine; but after their own lusts shall they heap to themselves teachers, having itching ears;**
> **And they shall turn away their ears from the truth, and shall be turned unto fables.**

See the moment you rebuke a believer - that is the last time you see them, yet by leaving they sign off their future. This all stems from despising the messengers God gave them but we need to look at what God says in Jeremiah 3 vs. 15;

...I will give you pastors after my own heart...

The word for your miracle comes through a person God chooses not the person you choose first then claim that "God told me" when you simply told and convinced yourself.

The prophecy comes to life

The good news from the lepers was communicated in the simplest way possible. It went from one person to another, until the news reached the king himself. Irregardless of who wanted to believe or who did not want to believe, Elisha's prophecy came to life for;

Then the people went out and plundered the tents of the Syrians. So a seah of fine flour was *sold* for a shekel, and two seahs of barley for a shekel, according to the word of the LORD.

When the good news that started with the report of the lepers was found to be true, there was no stopping the people. Because they knew their need, they were happy to receive God's provision to meet that need. The king's officer died. He not only died but died a terrible death:

2 Kings 7 vs.16 and **2 Kings 7 vs.17**
> **...the people trampled him in the gate, and he died,
> just as the man of God had said, who spoke when
> the king came down to him. So it happened just
> as the man of God had spoken to the king, saying,
> "Two seahs of barley for a shekel, and a seah of
> fine flour for a shekel, shall be sold tomorrow about
> this time in the gate of Samaria."**

The King's officer had answered the man of God, and said,
> **Now look, if the Lord would make windows in heaven,
> could such a thing be?" And he had said, "In fact, you
> shall see it with your eyes, but you shall not eat of it...**

The officer died, not because the people trampled him but because of unbelief. *Doubting God kills.* Doubting God short circuits the ability to take over the wealth of the wicked. It is a death sentence to doubt God.

When you feel you do not believe God know for a fact that is the devil's work and turn around and doubt the devil instead of God. God's love for His people is great enough that he summed it up in two words "only believe".

The wealth of the wicked is yours for the taking

The child of God ought to have God's best. A child of God was rich beyond his wildest imagination, way before he was even created. He was born into the right family. He was born where the money was and still is. He was born in a place of wealth created just for him.

Man wasn't created to be a slave, that is why favour follows him and that is exactly why the people who are not in the kingdom work for their money and heap up wealth without the knowledge that they are doing this heaping up of riches for the believer.

In short, the people on earth are all working for the child of God. Notice what God does:

Ecclesiastes 2 vs.26
> **...to the sinner God giveth travail to GATHER and
> HEAP UP riches that he may give to him that is
> a believer Of God.**

Act upon what the word of God says and you will amaze your world. You will be a person of plenty. You will become a wealth magnet. Your wealth will be wealth with a mission, Wealth to spread the Gospel with.

This revelation is not the truth you simply need to know for revelation is not the truth you simply know but the truth you use.

When you take *the wealth of the wicked,* your money will be money with a mission. The wealth of the wicked is up for grabs by those that love God!